JALIL KASTO

INTERNATIONAL LAW SERIES NO. 3

MODERN INTERNATIONAL LAW OF THE ENVIRONMENT

FIRST EDITION

KALL KWIK KINGSTON

INTERNATIONAL LAW SERIES NO.3

MODERN INTERNATIONAL LAW OF THE ENVIRONMENT

Jalil KASTO

Edited and Published by The Author
67 Lyncroft Gardens, Hounslow TW3 2QU U.K.
Tel: 081-898 2980

Copyright © Jalil Kasto 1995
All rights reserved. No part of this book
can be reproduced, stored in a retrieved system
or transmitted in any form by any means, electronic,
mechanical, photocopying, recording or translation,
or otherwise without the prior permission of the
copyright owner - the Author.

British Library Cataloguing in Publication Data
Modern International Law of the Environment
KASTO Jalil
ISBN 0 9517713 2 9
First Edition

Typeset by Abel Fischer Secretaries
127 Chiltern Drive, Surbiton, Surrey KT5 8LS
Tel. 081-390 8732
Printed in Kall Kwik Centre
179 Clarence Street, Kingston KT1 1QT
Tel. 081-541 0982

CONTENTS

			Page
Abbreviations			VIII
Introduction			1

Chapter 1	-	**The Environment as Human Concern**	5
Section 1	-	Emergence of the Environment Concept	5
A	-	Man Faces Nature	5
B	-	The Need for Environmental Awareness	5
C	-	The Divine Law	6
1.	-	The Jewish Faith	7
2.	-	The Green Christianity	7
3.	-	The Moslem Religion	8
D	-	The Formation of Earliest Norms	8
E	-	The Positive Law	10
Section 2	-	The Earth as a Global Problem	11
A	-	The Need for Cooperation	13
B	-	Creation of International Legal Norms	15

Chapter 2	-	**Protection of the Environment**	18
Section 1	-	Within State's Jurisdiction	18
A	-	The State	18
1.	-	The Legislation (Law)	19
a.	-	Conservation of Nature	19
	-	i. Protection of Wildlife, ii. Preservation of Living Resources, iii. Protection of Wild Birds	20
		iv. Other Animals, v. Plants,	20
		vi. Habitat	21
b.	-	Disposal of Waste	22
		i. Waste Management, ii. Meaning of Waste,	23
		iii. Control of Waste	24
		iv. Waste Authorities	25
		v. Licences	26
		vi. Civil Liability for Damage	27
		vii. Council of Europe Convention on Civil Liability	27
	a.	Main Principles	28
	b.	Total and Partial Liability and Disputes between Operators	28
	c.	Exemption from Liability	29
	d.	The Convention Applies to Damage After its Enforcement	29

		e.	Recourse against Third Party, f. Compensation	29
		g.	Jurisdiction, h. Time Bar	31
		viii. Recycling and Planning		31
	c.	-	Human Environment	32
		i. Public Safety and Health		33
		ii. Work Environment		34
		iii. Food and the Protection of the Consumers		37
		1. - The Quality of Food and its Protection		37
		a. Food Hygiene, B. Protection of Food		37
		c. Food Law		38
		d. The Availabiilty of Food		39
		2 - Protection of the Consumers		40
		i. EEC Directive on Product Liability		40
		ii. Product Liability Act		40
	d.	-	Noise and Nuisance	41
	e.	-	Pollution	43
		i. What is Pollution		43
		ii. UK Acts on Pollution		45
	f.	-	Water	45
		i. Water Acts in the UK		44
		ii. Rivers,		45
		iii. EEC Water Directives		46
		a. Drinking Water,		46
		b. Bathing Water		47
B.	-	The Individual		47
C.	-	Industrial Enterprises, Corporations and Firms		49
Section 2	-	The Role of the International Community		49
A.	-	The UN and Other International Organizations		50
1.	-	UN System		50
2.	-	EEC		52
B.	-	The Universal Action		53
Section 3	-	The Use of Technology		53
A.	-	Exchange of Technological Information and Experience		53
B.	-	Exploiting the Technological Advance		55

Chapter 3	-	**The Threat Against The Environment**	57
Section 1	-	Pollution	57
A	-	Air Pollution	57
1.	-	What is Air Pollution?	57
2.	-	Range of Air Pollution	57
3.	-	Causes of Air Pollution	58
	-	i. The Smoke, ii. Acid Rain, iii. Means of Transport, iv. Petrochemical Smog, v. The Ozone	58
		vi. Other Gases and Materials	59
4.	-	International Measures Against Air Pollution	59
5.	-	Duties of the Parties	60
6.	-	EEC Directives	60
B	-	Sea Pollution	60
1.	-	Definition	61
2.	-	What Causes Sea Pollution?	62
3.	-	The Law of Sea Pollution	62
		a. General Principles, b. Particular Principles	62
		i. The Binding Effects,	62
		ii. Territoriality, iii. Principle of Cooperation, iv. Setting Up Fund or Centre,	63
		v. Regulations for the Navigation of Ships and Carriage of Oil	63
		vii. Using of Technology and Scientific Research	63
4.	-	The Protection of Marine Living Resources	63
C	-	Land Pollution	63
		a. Urban Life (Particularly Populated and Industrial Cities, b. Waste	64
		c. Chemical, Toxin Pullutants and Insecticides, d. Bad Agriculture	65
Section 2	-	Nuclear Tests, Explosion and Contamination	66
A	-	Nuclear Radiation in the Atmosphere	66
1.	-	Radioactive Materials	66
2.	-	The Control of and Protection Against Radioactivity	66
3.	-	Nuclear Tests and Explosion in the Atmosphere	67
		i. The Treaty Banning Nuclear Weapons Test and Explosion	67
		ii. Protection of Outer Space	67
		iii. Preventing the Spread of Nuclear Weapons and Protection Against the Danger of Nuclear War	68
4.	-	Contamination of the Atmosphere	68
		i. The Nuclear Waste	68
		ii. Greenhouse Gases Emission	69

B	-	Explosion in the Sea Bed	69
1.	-	The Treaty Banning Nuclear Weapons Test in the Atmosphere, Outer Space and Under Water	69
2.	-	The Treaty on the Prohibition of the Emplacement of Nuclear Weapons and Other Weapons of Mass Destruction on the Sea-Bed and Ocean Floor and in Subsoil Thereof	70
C	-	Accidents in Nuclear Energy Plants and Nuclear Weapons	70
1.	-	The Convention on Early Notification of a Nuclear Accident	71
2.	-	The Convention on Assistance in the Case of a Nuclear Accident or Radiological Emergency	71
3.	-	Protection of Nuclear Material Against Accidents	72
4.	-	Liability for Nuclear Damage	72
		i. Principles of Liability	72
		a. Relating to Installation,	72
		b. Regarding the Nuclear Materals	73
		ii. Joint Liability of Operators, iii. Exoneration of Liability	73

Section 3	-	**Dumping**	74
A.	-	**Land Dumping**	74
B.	-	**Sea Dumping**	74
1.	-	Control of Dumping	74
		a. Waste and Matters Prohibited from Dumping	75
		b. Dumping by Special Permit	75
		c. Dumping by General Permit	75
2.	-	Measures for Ships and Aircraft	75
C.	-	International Conventions on Dumping	75
1.	-	Focus on the Convention on the Law of the Sea	75
2.	-	The Ban of Dumping and the States	76

Chapter 4	-	**Legal Responsibility and Disputes**	77
Section 1	-	The Emergence of Legal Responsibility	77
A.	-	The Legal System of Liability	77
1.	-	The Convention on the Law of the Sea	77
2.	-	Other International Conventions	78
B.	-	Principles of Liability	78
1.	-	Liability of the States from Enforcement Measures	78
2.	-	The Civil Liability	78

Section 2	-	**Regulation of Disputes**	79
A.	-	Methods of Settlement of Disputes	79
B.	-	Voluntary Methods	79
1.	-	Negotiation	79
2.	-	Mediation	79
3.	-	Conciliation	80
4.	-	Arbitration	80
		a. Arbitration Proceedings	80
		b. Applicable Law	81
C.	-	The Compulsory Jurisdiction of the Court	81
1.	-	The Compulsory Jurisdiction of the ICJ	81
2.	-	The Law of the Sea Tribunal	82
3.	-	The European Court of Justice (ECJ)	82
Section 3	-	**Compensation**	82
A.	-	The Basis of Compensation	82
B.	-	Conditions of Compensation	83
1.	-	Damage is Caused	83
2.	-	The Liability	83
3.	-	State Responsibility	83
4.	-	Time Bar	83
C.	-	Assessment of Compensation	83

Conclusion 85
New Environmental Glossary 87
Bibliography 93
Annexes
    1. - Convention on Biodiversity 95
    2. - Convention on Climate Change 116
Index

ABBREVIATIONS

AJIL	American Journal of International Law
APFS	Advisory Panel on Food Security
Art(s).	Article(s)
BDC	Biodiversity Convention
C.	Convention
CA	Court of Appeal
CCC	Climate Change Convention
CFCs	Chlorofluorocarbons
CoE	Council of Europe
CO_2	Carbon Dioxide
COPA	Control of Pollution Act (1974)
D	Directive
DoE	Department of the Environment
DoT	Department of Transport
EAECT	European Atomic Energy Community Treaty
EAWG	Environment Audit Working Group
ECA	Economic Commission for Africa
ECE	Economic Commission for Europe
ECJ	European Court of Justice
EEC	European Community
EECC	European Community Commission
EPA	Environmental Protection Act (1990)

EURATOM	European Atomic Energy Community
FAO	Food and Agriculture Organization
GA	General Assembly (UN)
GATT	General Agreement on Tariffs and Trade
GEMS	Global Environmental Monitoring System
HC	High Court
IBRD	International Bank for Reconstruction and Development
ICSU	International Council of Scientific Unions
ICJ	International Court of Justice
ILO	International Labour Organization
IMO	International Maritime Organization
IPCC	Inter-Governmental Panel on Climate Change
LWDAC(s)	Local Waste Authorities Contractor(s)
NCC(s)	National Conservation Council(s)
NGO(s)	Non-Governmental Organization(s)
NRA	National Rivers Authority
OAU	Organization of African Unity
OECD	Organization for Economic Cooperation & Development
Para(s).	Paragraph(s)
PCA	Planning & Compensation Act
S.	Section
SSSI	Site of Special Scientific Interest
TCPA	Town & Country Planning Act (1991)
TLR	Times Law Report

UN	United Nations Organization
UNCED	United Nations Conference on Environment and Development
UNCOD	United Nations Conference on Desertification
UNCTAD	United Nations Conference on Trade and Development
UNGEFDP	United Nations Global Environment Facility Development Programme
UNEP	United Nations Environment Programme
UNESCO	United Nations Educational, Scientific and Cultural Organization
UK	United Kingdom
US	United States
WCIP	World Climate Impact Studies Programme
WCED	World Commission on Environment & Development
WCS	World Conservation Strategy
WHO	World Health Organization
WMO	World Meteorological Organization
WRA	World Regulation Authority
WTO	World Trade Organization
WWF	Worldwide Fund for Nature

INTRODUCTION

Modern International Law of the Environment is the third book of the Series of International Law, which is a step forward for the continuity of the publication of original studies of modern international law.

It is very useful and interesting to publish this book which helps undoubtedly in the understanding of the recent development of international law.

There is no doubt that no important subject has gained more universal support and concern as the environmental problems.

Over the last two decades, the Green movements all over the world have become great pressure groups for the protection of our Earth, they regarded the environment as life for all peoples everywhere. The writers and the authors are very encouraged by the universal interest in the environment issues. Peoples want good environment, in order to live a good life, to have good food, enough cloths, so that they can eat well and warm themselves and enjoy good living.

Nobody can say that all the population of the world are happy with their environment.

The Earth as a global problem needs care. This care cannot be individual, societal, local, geographical or continental, but needs to be global which must be more cooperative that has to lay rules of harmonization for the activities of States in and out of their national jurisdiction to safeguard the protection of the environment against pollution, acid rain, natural disasters and nuclear contamination on the one hand, and to coordinate and regulate their cooperation with each other internationally on the other hand.

All peoples and countries of the world must bear their share in the care and the protection of the Earth.

The cooperation in the environmental issues as the universal Conference of Rio de Janeiro envisaged, is very necessary and essential in order to solve the problems of the environment all over the world.

Therefore, international law of the environment is the framework of the norms which regulate the activities of States, Governments, individuals (including corporate bodies) in the sphere of environment.

This law is very important and necessary. Every reader wants to study and understand the environmental law. The environment is strongly connected with development. The law is everyone's teeth in order to eat and easily digest, so when he/she knows the law, they can understand their rights and obligations. Law confers rights and puts obligations and responsibilities on States and individuals to protect themselves from the dangers which threaten the environment. International law of the environment is the legal instruments and the biding environmental norms for the protection of the environment that ensure cooperation of States and peoples in order to make safe haven for all peoples.

Modern international law of the environment protects the interests of the poor countries which need help and assistance in order to bear their responsibilities and contribute to the protection of the environment.

To deal with the environment necessitates to deal with the law, as it involves the norms which protect the environment, ensure the means and resources for the conservation of biodiversity species, improve the habitat, combat the pollution and contamination of land, sea and atmosphere and enhance the cooperation of the members of the international community.

The environment needs this law, because it guarantees the involvement of the members of the international community in the cooperation for the protection of the Earth from hazards and dangers that can be prevented by this cooperation on one hand, and by taking the measures

Introduction

which combat the pollution of environment which affects other countries on the other hand. Modern international law of the environment does not only involve the cooperation of States internationally, but also binds them within their jurisdiction to cooperate with the international community as a whole in order to ensure the universal cooperation for the protection of the environment. This means that international law of the environment has to play a big role in the protection of the environment globally.

Although there are great efforts and cries over all the world for the protection and the care for the environment, and many States and international organizations call for a concerted international actions and cooperation in dealing with the environmental issues. But still these efforts and concerns lag behind what would be expected in this concern.

The preamble of the International Climate Change Convention signed at Rio de Janeiro on 5 June 1992 stresses this fact by saying "Change in the Earth climate and its adverse effects are a common concern of humankind". In this brief sentence, the problems and dangers which face the environment affect all the international community.

Although international law of the environment has been developing since the creation of the UN, but its emergence as a distinct modern international law took place in the UN Conference on Human Environment at Stockholm 5-16 June 1972.

This Conference has laid down the basic principles of this law. This Conference stressed the great human role in the transformation of the environment, although it is relatively less effective than the forces of nature, as it says; "Man has acquired the power to transform his environment in countless ways and on an unprecedented scale". The Stockholm Conference put the fundamental principles of this law and urged the international community to cooperate, using technology and science for the transformation of the environment, especially, the quality of life of the human environment.

This concern does not involve the States, international organizations, inter-governmental or non-governmental only, but also individuals, industrial, economic firms and enterprises that must bear their responsibilities and cooperate in the environmental protection, so that the protection of the Earth would be universal that involves all peoples all over the world. The international concern about the environment affected and strengthened the green movements all over the world.

It is very advantageous that food chains like Safeway, Sainsbury's, Gateway (Somerfield), Tesco, Waitrose and others are paying great attention to environmental issues and participating in the international action for the environment facing the challenges which concern all humankind. International law of the environment is an effective and active instrument of cooperation on worldwide environmental challenges. It is a means of harmony of international actions for the protection of the environment.

International law of the environment as distinct rules of international law is very modern, because its rules and norms were recently established, especially in the last three decades where the international public opinion all over the world and the peoples began to understand the necessity of the protection of the Earth, their national resources, the animals and the plants, the habitat, to conserve the diversity of species and to improve the quality of life.

The international concern about the environment reflected again in the activities of the UN and its specialized organizations which have active role in environmental protection; like the UNEP and UNCED. These activities led to the adoption of 142 conventions in the last twenty years, more than twice the number of international conventions which were concluded in the fifty years

Introduction

before 1972.

The international conventions on the environmental issues form great norms and principles of modern international law of the environment. They have enriched this law by increasing its rules and sphere of application.

On the other hand, the national legislations of States play a big role in the application and implementation of its rules in their jurisdiction, where they became very effective at both national and international levels.

The most important development of international law of environment is the UN Conference on Environment and Development held at Rio de Janeiro (June 3-14) 1992, in which the two UN specialized organizations on environment, UNEP and UNCED played their important role together with 200 States, the largest number of States in the history attended this Conference and other Governmental and NGOs, agencies, groups and individuals, having interests in the Earth Summit.

Mr Boutros Ghali, the Secretary General of the UN, stressed the necessity to conclude a political and ethical contract with nature - this Earth - to which we owe our existence and which gives us sustenance, and the maintenance of the spirit of Rio which creates a pattern of behaviour[1] While the Secretary General of UNCED regarded this Summit as great epoch in history, especially concerning the UN and the world community.[2]

In this introduction, it should be emphasised that the Earth Summit of Rio de Janeiro is a significant codification of the principles of international law of the environment after the Stockholm Conference (1972). The two significant international conventions on Climate Change and on Biological Diversity[3], and other documents, as the Agenda 21, Forest Principles are great achievement in the creation of global partnership in the international cooperation for the build up of effective international law of the environment.

The Braer (tanker) disaster which took place on 5 January 1993 at the southern tip of The Shetlands, when the tanker's engine failed in a 90mph storm. It caused one of the greatest environmental disasters in history.

The pollution of the sea, the coast and the death of thousands of birds and animals in the region call upon the entire international community to cooperate in solidarity in order to prevent the occurrence of such a disaster.

The disaster stresses the role of international law of environment and its effective normative standards to control the suitability of the tankers to go on seas and to impose more restrictive measures in order to protect the environment which is the concern of all international communities.

The other sea pollution caused by the spillage of oil from the Greek tanker near the Spanish coast, which exploded after it collided with rocks and spilled on 21.2.1992. It was estimated that it caused £330m damage to the marine environment as a result of 8 million gallons of oil spilling into the sea which caused the death of thousands of birds and animals.

This environmental disaster and others put the focus on the necessity of ensuring more international cooperation for the protection of the environment and the respect for the international law of the environment and imposing more restrictive standards for the control of

---

[1] - UN Conference on Environment and Development. Securing the Future. Geneva. 1992. P. 1.
[2] - Ibid..
[3] - Their texts are published completely in the Annexes.

Introduction

oil tankers and their suitability for shipping.

The danger of pollution is not a threat against one country, but also threatens all countries and the world community as a whole. So in considering the importance of international law of the environment is very necessary in regard to its impact on the international community which faces many environmental issues which widen its scope and the area of its application. This Book is a comprehensive study which concentrates on the important issues and subjects which are very necessary to explain in the light of the recent development of the law.

The study took into account the recent changes and trends of legal concepts which have been taking place in the last two decades, especially, the adoption of a great number of international conventions on the environment.

So the plan involves 4 chapters:

1 -   The Environment as Human Concern
2 -   Protection of the Environment
3 -   The Threat against the Environment
4 -   Environmental Legal Responsibilities and Disputes.

Each of the chapters includes many issues, subjects and topics which are necessary to study in order to match the demand for a modern study on this subject and to meet the international concern about the environment, especially after the Earth Summit at Rio de Janeiro.

The Book also includes the full texts of the Conventions on Climate Change and Biological Diversity and other useful texts, besides an environmental glossary.

So the Book is a good step forward in the study of international law of the environment and its development.

London   Jalil KASTO

Chapter 1

THE ENVIRONMENT AS HUMAN CONCERN

The environment is the surroundings of life and the effective factor which affects the ecosystem and ecology. Life cannot exist without the good protecting environment.[1]

Since the creation, the environment, or the natural surroundings were the most effective factor which influenced the action, behaviour and thinking of humankind.

The first human concept about the environment was the mother Earth the natural home of the earliest man who had struggled to protect himself against the unkind nature, and to find the means and ways to ensure his living and the living of animals and plants which he used for his subsistence.

Section 1 - Emergence of the Environmental Concept

The earliest man imagined the natural phenomena are the main factors which affected his environment. So he considered the sun, the atmosphere, the clouds, the wind, the sea and the fire are the great forces which affected his life and thus by his primitive thinking and means he tried to protect himself against the forces of nature. Besides, he struggled to protect himself against the beasts and to tame the animals which he thought were necessary to his living and to grow the plants which he used for his food.

A - Man faces Nature

The earliest man faced nature with fear and curiosity. He didn't know the mystery of this curious universe and the natural forces. His main problem was how he, as a weak creature, could resist the forces of nature and how to protect himself by making the shelter to warn his body by using primitive materials as plant leaves and animal skins to clothe himself and caring for his food.

B - The Need for Environmental-Awareness

The earliest man, despite his primitiveness, was conscious of the environmental dangers which he always faced with challenges and fears.
He was in fact a slave of the environment and its hazards affected his thinking. The environment appeared in the ways and means of his living, his shelter (the cave), his food and the type of his social relations in the earliest days, whether inside the family, the tribe, the community, the city or the ancient State.
So he had environmental awareness, which had an impressive impact on his fears and challenges of nature.

---

[1] - The recent Council of Europe Convention on "Civil Liability for Damage Resulting from Activities Dangerous to the Environment" of 21.6.93, defines the "environment" Art.2(10): . natural resources both abiotic and biotic, such as air, water, soil, fauna and flora and the interaction between the same factors; . property which forms part of the cultural heritage; and . the characteristic aspects of the landscape".

C - The Divine Law

The phenomena of the natural forces affected the earliest man and attracted his attention, through the earliest civilizations, and raised his fears, worries and thinking about the natural and physical order which governs the Earth and the universe.

In the literature of the old civilizations we find many writings and poems about the effect of the environment since the creation of the universe and the Earth. And although the ancient religions before the Jewish, Christian and Moslem religions did not believe in eternal, immortal and holy God the creator, but their gods symbolize the forces of nature which affect the environment.

In Rig Veda collection of hymns (2000-1500 BC) of the ancient Hindu religion, there is an environmental creation, where there were the sky, the space, the water and darkness, nothing else existed and there was an emptiness.

No one knows how the creation happened, perhaps, by heat and afterwards the gods came. Perhaps, the environmental change happened by the effect of waters. When man came on Earth, he was the ruler of immortality and the greatest of all creatures. He grows beyond everything through food and all other creatures are beyond him. Human beings formed three quarters of all creatures which were one quarter.

The Rig Veda speaks of life cycle and death on mother Earth which is the world of light and renewal. Heaven is the place of rest and happiness.

The Agni (fire) is god of sacrificial fire, the burning of body fire, lighting and the sun. The body will disperse into the sky, earth and water. The sun gives light and heat.

The life cycle, begins with the birth and ends by death, but death is the renewal of life to all creatures, humans, inhumans, and plants which are essential for the living of man.[1]

Also many ancient philosophers studied the natural phenomena and their deep dimensions on the environment.

The Greek philosophers were the first to present an empirical explanation, among the best of them was the great philosopher Aristotle who viewed the universe affects the atmosphere which surrounds the Earth, and so the environment is subject to change, this is because the elements of weather generate a change, this appears in the phenomena of clouds, thunder, rain, snow, frost and dew.[2]

The Aristotelian theory of the environment was based on the causes of circular motion that stood on the perception of Aristotle about the universe, the natural order, life and the environment. Aristotle depended on observation and philosophical consideration in expressing his views.

Also Aristotle thought of God was immaterial, his activities are intellectual and he is the thinking of thinking.

Aristotle believed that god must be actively alive, a big being, eternal, perfect in goodness, life and duration, continuous and eternal. That is what God is.[3]

Aristotle said that animals, plants are also alive and share the nutrition and reproduction as humans.

---

[1] - **Rig Veda** Translation of Wendy Deniger O'Flanherty. Penguin Books. 1981. PP. 25-40.
[2] - Jonathan Barnes - **Aristotle**. Oxford University Press. PP. 61-62.
[3] - V.Luce. **Introduction to Greek Philosophy.** Thames and Hudson, 92. PP. 123-128.

He saw the motion of heavens is determined by the necessity and described the natural world as continuous, eternal, regular in continuous change.[1]

On the other hand, the three heavenly religions which believe in one mighty God, the creator of heaven and Earth agree that the powerful God is the ruler of the environment. And so, it is necessary to study their attitudes towards the environment.

1. The Jewish Faith

Many verses in the Old Testament support the idea that God can change the environment, and man cannot resist the will of God.[2] God will reward man for his obedience and punish him for his disobedience and the environmental change is in the hand of God.[3] And so as it appears from the scriptures, the environment is under the command of God.[4]

According to Isaiah, man must follow the directions of God in order to protect the environment and to have the right in life.[5]

2. The Green Christianity

Christianity worships God the creator, the loving, kind and protecting Lord of the people and the environment.

The Christian faith is based on the belief in the power of God and the essence of God reflects goodness, mercy, love and fairness. Jesus Christ said: "Love God, your father and mother and your neighbour.' Jesus' message to all humankind to do good and to be hostile to evil.

These are the basic principles of the divine law concerning the environment, the care for neighbour, goodness for surroundings, and care for the protection of the environment (do not do evil). These are the basic greens of the Christian environmental principles. Anyhow, the good environment is an endowment of the loving God, and his power to keep it well.[6]

Man cannot act in defiance of God, regarding nature. The act of God is irresistible. Man should be ready to do whatever is good, concerning the environment.[7] Whatever man can have a power of invention, is unable to expect what nature would involve,[8] despite the exploitation of science and technology nowadays.

According to the eternal law, Christianity regards the environment is under God's protection,

---

[1] - Ibid. P. 63

[2] - **Leviticus 25/23,** the Lord said to Moses: "...the land is mine and you are, but aliens and my tenants'. 26/4 "I will send you rain in its season and the ground will yield its crops and the trees in field their fruits."

[3] - **Leviticus, 26/8,** 'and I will give peace in the land.'. Deuteronomy. 12/1 'these are the decrees and laws you must be careful to follow in the land of the Lord, the God of your father, has given you to possess... and occupy all your earthly life.' David Psalm 24/1, 'The Earth is the Lord's, and everything in it, the world, and all who live in it, for he founded it upon the seas and established upon waters.'

[4] - **Psalm 46,** 'He lifts his voice the Earth melts.'

[5] - **Isaiah. 45/12-13.** 'I have made the Earth and created man upon it. I have raised him up in righteousness and I will direct all his ways, he shall build my city.' **Jeremiah 32/17.** 'Sovereign Lord, you have made the heavens and the Earth by your great power and stretched arm. Nothing is too hard for you.'

[6] - **Paul, Corinthians. 10/26** 'The Earth is the Lord's and everything in it.'

[7] - **Paul, Titus 3/1.** 'Be ready to do whatever is good'.

[8] - **John 3/8.** 'The wind blows where it pleases, You can hear its sound, But you cannot tell where it comes from, or where it is going' Jesus. Scientists expectations in many times about the earthquakes and volcanoes were wrong. Thousands of victims fell as a result of them, in addition to the destruction they caused.

Emergence of the Environmental Concept

man should pray God always to keep the nature well and kind and to protect the humankind from evil and mishap.

On the other hand, man should care for the environment, do good for his neighbours and protect the environment and do not evil or harm to others, whether humans or other creatures. Jesus said: 'You must be on watch and alert'. So spiritual watch as well as material watch are essential for the protection and care for the environment.[1]

So the green values are Christian values.

iii   The Moslem Religion

There are many verses in the Koran regarding the environment. God has power to create, and heaven and Earth are his own.[2] God has power to make the environment safe for humankind.[3] Islam as well as Christianity call upon man to be fair and kind towards the environment, and to do what he can in order to protect the environment.

D - The Formulation of Earliest Norms

Both nature and the environmental Divine Law formed the earliest norms of environmental law. So the role of man was weak in affecting the environmental change and was solely self-protective or with regard to the family and the tribe. The concept of this protection was primitive, as the means and methods were not so effective to change the environment for the benefit of man. Man relied on rites, spiritual and religious traditions and praying God to protect the environment and to make it convenient for living.

The environmental consciousness in the earliest ages of humankind was motivated by fear of natural forces, which affect the environment. So people at that times worshipped the sun, the sea, the wind, the clouds and rain, regarded them as gods.

Moreover, all their actions were protective, they gained experience from the environmental phenomena. So they adapted themselves to the environment, by primitive means, as living in places where they were suitable for natural shelters: as caves, or ground which is naturally protected from wind, rain, flood and natural changes which menaced their lives.

All their means of survival were primitive, but protective as regards the food, cloths and shelter, and so they adapted themselves to cooperative type of living, as it ensured for them some kind of protection against environmental threats and challenges.

The earliest norms of the environment were local and mostly in limited areas, where the human communities were very local and did not extend far enough, as the social, economic and external relations did not involve large communities. Although some great empires had been founded and the trade flourished, as the Assyrian, Persian, Phoenician and Roman empires, but they did not care for the environment, their only concern was the conquest and trade, especially with

---

[1] - **Christian Science Sentinel.** 20 April 1992, Vol.94, No.16. Responsibility for the Environment - A spiritual Watch. What I say unto you I say unto all, watch,' **Jesus.** The writer says that environmental planning, including planning for the unplanned. He stresses the New Testament calls for the alertness: 'Watch and pray.'

[2] - **Cow Surat. V.104.** 'Do you know heavens and Earth belong to God! Cow... V. 164 'God water the Earth and put life in it, after death and created all creatures, the clouds and the wind.'

[3] - **Cow .. V.22.** '(God) .. made the Earth your bed and shelter and bring rain from the sky, so that to produce fruits and food for you.

slaves. So they did not adopt an empirical policy in regard to the environment. Moreover, all human thinking at that stage of civilization was attached to the divine power which protects the environment. This thinking appears in the old India songs.[1]
Thus the primitive custom was based on worshipping the natural forces, and afterwards the holy God, regarding the Jewish, Christian and Moslem religions. The principles of the environmental law were religious and metaphysical, as the blessings of God, God save heaven and the Earth. Heaven cares for food, protection and prevents natural disasters.[2]
Whatever, the source of knowledge which created the environmental consciousness in the mind of man, whether God[3] or spontaneously the mind of man created this environmental consciousness by orientation or experience for the benefit of the progress and development.
There is no doubt that the earliest man was able to develop his **energies and thinking** for the environmental adaptability or to create within his locality, at the first stage of humankind civilization some changes on environment. This appears in the development of irrigation and agriculture in the earliest civilization in Mesopotamia and Egypt.
History tells us that the Babylonians and Egyptians have gone far enough in building canals, bridges and irrigation systems and the development of agriculture, growing grain that made the green fields and the environment suitable for their needs. Needless to say that when peoples began to contact each other either by emigration, conquest or peaceful relations, they benefitted from each others experience and progress. This of course has developed the environmental consciousness.
One cannot ignore the fact, that science and technology from the earliest stages of humankind civilization worked side by side with religions in order to effect an environmental consciousness. The increase of knowledge and the challenges the natural forces effect, led to more environmental awareness.
There is no doubt, that the effect of religion on the mind of humankind helped to increase the knowledge about the environment and the development of the environmental consciousness. Over centuries, environmental consciousness has been growing as environmental science became sine qua non of modern life. But despite the necessity for a positive law to regulate the environmental issues, the attempts to make environmental law lagged behind the necessity to regulate the different aspects of the environment.
Therefore the earliest environmental norms can be summarised:
1 - Environment is affected by divine power.
2 - Man neither affects the natural forces which affect the environment. Nor can he resist them.
3 - Self protection as a means against the environment.
4 - Goodness, fairness and care for neighbours are necessary for environmental consciousness.
5 - The growing need for living in societal shelters and housing which ensured for the people collective protection.

---

[1] - God is in the water, God in on the land, God is in the heart, God is in the forest, God is in the mountain, God is in the cave, God is in the Earth, God is in the heavens, God is here, God is there, God is in space, God is in time, God is invisible, God is without creed, God, you are in the river, You are in the sea, You are in the tree, You are in the leaves.
[2] - **Huzur Maharaj and Sawan Singh. Philosophy of the Masters.** Radha Soami Satsang Beas. 1973. pp. 190-194.
[3] - **2. Peter. 1/5.** For the very reason, make every effort to add to your faith goodness, and to goodness, knowledge, self-control, and to self-control perseverance. **(The New Testament).**

Emergence of the Environmental Concept

E - The Positive Law

The adoption of legislation on pollution, contamination and poisoning of the environment had not taken place until the sixties. During these years there has been concern inside and outside the State's jurisdiction to make positive domestic or international law on the environment.

One can find, as a result of industrial revolution social legislations concerning the industrial environment and environmental regulations about the conditions of work, health of workers and safety in factories and industrial enterprises, but they lagged behind the requirements of environmental concern in different aspects of life.

To make legislations to control the environment is a recent concept and this action whether by the State or by international community (bilateral, multilateral, organizational conventions) is very recent and has not happened, but only during the last three or four decades, where national and international legislations had been adopted.

A general law of environment in the legal terms, began to grow afterwards, and continued to develop on the national and international plain.

Environmental positive law as it is known nowadays was in complete absence and was a great vacuum of this law for centuries, until the economic and industrial awakening swept Europe in the eighteenth and nineteenth centuries. And when economic and social movements strengthened the environmental consciousness and the care for the environment became urgent, especially after many writers, philosophers and ecologists have published their books which dealt with the environmental protection.

The positive law in this concern, is both national and international law which needs law-making machinery either by the State or inter-States relations.

On the other hand, environmental law is preventative, protective, besides it has effects on living, whether humans, animals or plants, and involves the State, the individual and the international community. Therefore it is public law and has erga omnes effect.

So these considerations have not been estimated well, until science and technology have developed and produced their effects on the environment, whether for evil or good, and their impact on the environment has been effective. So this focuses on a great change in the attitude of humankind towards the environmental law.

Previously all environmental phenomena were believed they occur, either by divine power (God) or natural forces, beyond the human power and influence. But when science and technology have been exploited, their effect on the environment have been observed, so the human attitude towards them has been changed and the need for positive norms to regulate their use and to protect or prevent their damage or disadvantage to the individual, the State or the International community by law.

This result led to the importance of positive law with regard to the environment. So the environmental law began to grow and develop, especially in the last three decades.

The growing need to legislate on environmental issues, especially which concern public health, water, poisoning of foods, conservation, protection of forests, control of rivers from pollution, nuclear contamination of land, water and air and control of social conditions in factories and many other issues.

The growing pressure of green movements all over the world increased the call for the legislation of laws for the control, protection and improvement of the environment.

This has increased the importance of positive law for the regulation of environmental issues and problems and the protection of Mother Earth.

Needless to say that there is an interaction between national and international law. This is clear from the advance of the environmental protection by States which affected environmental law, and soon the domestic law reflects on international law, especially as concerns the environment, because it has a global concern, and does not affect one nation or one people, but it is the concern of all nations and peoples.

The environmental positive law has been growing by the protection of working environment and health and safety of workers in factories. This protection was relatively in a small environment, but the environmental consciousness throughout the world and the environmental protection have been growing and they resulted in a global movement.

This is clear from the growing movements of greens all over the world.

There are many States Acts which come under the ambit of positive law and reflect the many environmental issues, that give evidence on the importance of environmental law.

Since the fifties environmental positive law has been consolidated. Many States acts and legislations about the environmental issues reflect the importance of the protection and care for the environment, e.g. in the UK, the Shop Act (1950), Factories Act (1961) and Health and Safety at Work Act (1979).[1]

Also the Law of 1974 on Work Environment which was revised in 1978 in Sweden under the pressure of the environmentalists the Swedish Government acted this law for the health and safety of workers and intended humanizing the work environment.[2]

Moreover, international law of the environment affects the national law, the different international conventions on pollution, the protection of environment, conservation, protection of animals and plants etc., became part of national law in many countries which are parties to the conventions concerned.

And since the sixties, many countries have acted legislations on pollution and accepted the norms of pollution as agreed upon in international law of the environment in their legal order.[3]

So both domestic and international law increase the norms of environmental positive law, and thus the need to fill the gap which exists in the field of environmental positive law can be met.

Section 2 - The Earth as a Global Problem

"Recognising the integral and independent Nature of the Earth our home"
(The preamble of Agenda 21, UNCED)

The global problems of the environment in their totality are addressed to all countries and peoples of the world (that is the Earth as a whole), in this content, the global problems of the environment mean that all countries and peoples share the responsibility and rights which the global environment involves. This means the global partnership in caring for the environment. Over centuries, the peoples of the world suffered from their misunderstanding of the environmental problems and how to solve them and to use science and technology to protect the

---

[1] - Croner's Employment Law - Croner's Guide to Health and Safety. Croner's Publications Ltd, 2nd Ed. 1991. pp. 1,2,11,98

[2] - **Henry Milner. Sweden Social Democracy in Practice.** Oxford University Press. 90. p. 41.

[3] - See Control of Pollution Act (1974), replaced by Water Act (1989) and Environmental Protection Act (1990) in the U.K. Also, the Belgian Act on the Protection of Surface Waters against Pollution (1971) and Air Pollution Act (1964).

The Earth as a Global Problem

environment and to prevent the damage caused to it. And their misinterpretation of many natural phenomena which caused the many sufferings of peoples over centuries.

The belief that natural forces or divine power can only affect the environment, human cannot resist God's will and natural forces, in order to stop natural disasters or at least to have protection from natural hazards, so the growing advance of knowledge, science and technology, and the interest in environmental watch which was found very necessary and the increase in the desire for the sustenance of life for all living things on the Earth united the humankind efforts to look at the global environmental problems as one which relates to all peoples and nations of the Earth.

Combining all their efforts they began to feel that human attitudes towards the global environmental problems must be tackled regarding the protection of our Planet as a whole, and that humankind cannot stay put with regard to the harms and dangers caused to Mother Earth which hopefully ensures a kind environment for all living creatures.

Tackling the global problems necessitates the protection of the Earth and the sustenance of life and the control of the dangers and causes of the destruction of the environment and the natural disequilibrium by human conduct, actions, negligence and exploitation.

The international community has found that the global environment problems can be tackled by international cooperation in many fields, and that requires:

1 - **Stabilizing the natural ecosystems;**
2 - **Controlling desertification and destruction of forests;**
3 - **Controlling pollution (air, land and sea);**
4 - **Decreasing the emissions of harmful gases to the ozone layer and its protection in the atmosphere;**
5 - **Providing the means and resources for conservation of biological diversity;**
6 - **Economizing the use of energy and decreasing consumption which causes the Earth warming;**
7 - **Using biotechnology for the enhancement and improvement of the environment;**
8 - **Encouraging active and beneficial relations between humans and the environment locally, regionally and internationally;**
9 - **Protection of health from toxic chemicals, waste and control of dangerous sewage.**
10 - **Application of international strategy for the global environment and the protection of the Earth.**[1]

The protection of the planet which is the main common concern of humankind, especially in the last two decades. This common concern has led the UN and its specialized Organizations, the UNCED, UNEP, IMO and WMO to convene several international conferences on the protection of global environment and the development of international law of the environment, through the conclusion of various conventions, e.g. the C. for the protection of the Ozone layer (1985), the Montreal Protocol on Substances that deplete the Ozone layer (1987) amended on 29 June (1990).

The Climate Change Convention objectives are provided in Art. (2) which puts the international legal framework for the protection of global climate by stabilization of greenhouse gas concentrations in the atmosphere at a level that would prevent dangerous anthropogenic interference with the climate change. Such a level should be achieved within a time frame

---

[1] - UNCED - The Global Partnership for Environment and Development - Guide to Agenda 21. Geneva. 1992. pp. 62-88.

sufficient to allow ecosystems to adapt naturally to climate change.

Paras. (e,f,g and h) of Art 4 (Commitments of Climate Convention) provide that the Member-States cooperate in preparing for adaptation to the impacts of climate change, develop and elaborate appropriate and integral plans for coastal zone management, water resources and agriculture, and for the protection and rehabilitation of areas, particularly in Africa, affected by drought and desertification, as well as floods.

The Member-States take climate change considerations into account, to the extent feasible, in their relevant social, economic and environmental policies and actions, and employ appropriate methods, for example impact assessments, formulated and determined nationally, with a view to minimizing adverse effects on the economy, on public health and on the environment, of projects or measures undertaken by them to mitigate or adapt to climate change.

The Member-States promote and cooperate in scientific, technological, technical, social, economic and other research, systematic observation and development of data archives related to the climate system and intended to further the understanding and reduce or eliminate the remaining uncertainties regarding the causes, effects, magnitude and timing of climate change and the economic and social consequences of various response strategies; in addition to exchange of all kinds of information regarding the climate system and change and the cooperation in education, training and public awareness regarding the climate change. Experts on global environment have dealt with the protection of Mother Earth, 'our common future' in specifying these subjects, as the concern of humankind, and it is the task of the international community as a whole to deal with and cooperate for the benefit of human generations and the basis of intergenerational equity, forests, climate change, biodiversity, sustainable agriculture, waste management, including toxic and hazardous areas and legal financial arrangements.[1]

A - The Need for Cooperation

Uniting the efforts of all nations and peoples of the international community for the protection of Mother Earth is an essential task of the international community as a whole. The problems which face the global environment; like ozone depletion, warming, pollution, acid rain, conservation and biological diversity are universal, they create great dangers to Mother Earth and thus, tackling them needs every effort from the international community, regardless of the geographical situation, the economic resources and the degree of development.

The global cooperation of all peoples in the international community is necessary in order to secure the protection of Mother Earth.

International cooperation is the legal and political foundation for any arrangements to meet the problems which threaten the global environment and the security of Mother Earth. For this reason, the Rio International Conference on Environment regarded the international cooperation is the prime task of all nations, and on this basis the UNCED Declaration stated in its principles that all peoples and States should cooperate for the benefit of global environment.[2]

Principles 11 and 15 of the Stockholm Declaration on 15 December 1972 state that States' environmental policies should achieve environmental benefits for all and avoid environmental

---

[1] - The Irish Times on 19.5.1992.
[2] - Principle 7: States shall cooperate in a spirit of global partnership to conserve, protect and restore the health and integrity of the Earth's ecosystem .... UNCED. The Global Partnership. Geneva 1992. pp. 1-2.

damage and dangers which threaten the environment and the aim of these policies must be the cooperation for the improvement and protection of the environment.

Also principle 24 of the same Declaration stressed the cooperative spirit of all countries in their policies, activities, unilaterally, bilaterally and multilaterally to prevent, reduce and eliminate adverse environmental effects resulting from activities conducted in all spheres.[1]

Also the preamble of the UN Convention on Biological Diversity concluded in Rio (1992) stressed the importance of cooperation among States and other NGOs for the conservation of biological diversity. Art. 5 of this Convention stressed the cooperation which is regarded a 'duty' on each country (State obligation in respect of areas beyond national jurisdiction) for conservation and sustainable use of biological diversity.[2]

The Climate Change Convention, for its part has stressed the importance of cooperation for the benefit of the global environment, where its preamble calls for "the widest possible cooperation by all countries and their participation in an effective and appropriate international response". Besides, Paras g, h, i, j of Art. 4 (commitments) provided for the fullest cooperation in the fields of science, technology, research data, data exchange on climate change, training, public awareness and participation, concerning climate change.[3]

The Rio Summit stressed the importance of environmental cooperation and its Agenda 21 gave new meaning to this cooperation by calling it 'Global Partnership' in order to foster a climate of genuine cooperation and solidarity.

This global partnership involves the harmonization of national and international policies of States, the international organizations, NGOs, multinational corporations and individuals efforts for the purpose of environmental cooperation.[4]

But cooperation would be just an oral or written word on paper without achieving its objectives. The objectives of global cooperation are global partnership of all States and peoples and fulfilment of States obligations.

Cooperation necessitates ensuring the enforcement of all international and legal conventions and agreements dealing with environmental matters. This involves participation and compliance with regard to States obligations, in order to secure the protection of Mother Earth and the environmental security.

Also cooperation necessitates the fulfilment of all international agreements and institutional arrangements at national, sub-regional, regional and international institutional levels and the cooperation with the UN Systems as well as inter-governmental and NGOs and the private sector.[5]

Therefore, cooperation needs to be translated to practical coordination and participation of all countries and peoples individually and collectively to implement the requirements of environmental necessities, in order to protect the Mother Earth and to put into action all measures to avoid the environmental dangers and to meet all the environmental challenges at international level. Poor and rich countries must understand that their interests individually are

---

[1] - Principle 24 of the Stockholm Declaration: International matters concerning the protection and the improvement of the environment should be handled in a cooperative spirit by all countries, big and small, on an equal footing. Cooperation through multilateral or bilateral arrangements or other appropriate means is essential ...
[2] - See the Convention in the Annexes.
[3] - See the text. Ibid.
[4] - UNCED. Securing the Future. Geneva. 1992. p. 2.
[5] - UNCED. Global Partnership. Geneva. 1992. p. 106.

realized by achieving the interests of all the international community for the benefit of the global environment and facing the dangers and challenges collectively. Any lack of cooperation in solving the environmental issues affects the international community as a whole.

The environmental cooperation necessitates the establishment of international mechanism for the cooperation which can work to achieve the purposes of environmental strategies and implement Agenda 21 that intends the full cooperation in all fields, technological, technical, social, economic and political at all levels.

B - Creation of International Legal Norms

It has been previously explained that the environment is a global problem and the protection of Mother Earth is a challenge facing all the international community. For this reason the need to formulate international norms stems from the necessity for legal norms accepted by States and have binding effects on them. So that there would be legal obligations concerning their cooperation that involves all the environmental problems, inter alia, avoiding the dangers and hazards of the environment or any damage or injury which is caused by a member of the international community to another member. Therefore cooperation needs legal instruments to regulate the practice of the States, in their relations with each other or the machinery to create these norms and which by repetition become custom that applies to similar circumstances and the States may voluntarily accept or adhere to it. On this basis the international legal norms formulate, whether customary or treaty law and develop simultaneously and constantly in the environmental relations between States.

The Smetler Arbitration case (1941) between US-Canada confirms that States apply voluntarily environmental norms which benefit their interests, without prior agreement. Moreover the Tribunal confirmed the existence of principles of international law of the environment as well American positive law, and both agreed that (no State has the right to use or permit the use of its territory in such a manner as to cause injury by fumes which were caused by the emission of sulphur dioxide from the Canadian Smetler, which were across the border into the US territory, or the properties or person therein, when the case is of serious consequence and the injury is established by clear and convincing evidence.[1]

The Tribunal concluded that the State has a duty to protect other States against acts caused by individuals (or firms) within its jurisdiction.[2]

Moreover, national courts and the ICJ have developed the principles of international law of the environment in many cases.

In the Corfu case (UK v Albania, 1949) the ICJ regarded the elementary considerations of humanity put obligation on each State not to use its territory to cause damage to other States rights.[3]

International environmental law like the general international law has developed and been

---

[1] - The Arbitral Tribunal in the Smetler case said: "It is, therefore, the duty of the Government of the Dominion of Canada to see to it that this conduct should be in conformity with the obligation of the Dominion under international law as herein determined ...". **Martin Dixon & Robert McCorquodale. Cases and Materials on International Law**. Blackstone Press. 1991. p. 453.

[2] - **David Ott. Public International Law**. Pitman 1987. p. 291. The author said that a Swiss case preceeded the decision of the Tribunal of the Smetler and was the legal ground of this decision.

[3] - **ICJ. The Corfu Case**. Dixon and McCorquodale. Ibid. p. 453.

developing and growing by the principles and maxims of judicial decisions, States practices, treaty law and doctrine.

The embryonic development of environmental law began with a number of judicial decisions and continued to grow rapidly after the second world war since the creation of the UN and its family Organizations. There is no doubt that the Smetler case and other judicial decisions between contesting parties have no erga omnes effect, unless the case affects the international community or the global environment, although it may produce legal effect on the doctrine and other courts jurisprudence. That depends on the degree of appreciation. Nevertheless, the environmental awareness at global level has affected the creation of international legal norms through more effective means, especially when there is need for these norms either through treaty law, or international organizations and especially the UNEP, UNCED, GATT, FAO, IMO, WCIP, WMO and WWF.

The development of international legal norms, although was steady through the last three decades and especially since the Stockholm Declaration (1972), but this development lagged behind the need for care to global environment.

One cannot ignore the jurisprudence of the ICJ in two cases where it considered the protection of the environment is a duty towards the international community.[1]

On the other hand, there were other obstacles to tackle the environmental issues. These appear in the difference on necessities between the poor and the rich countries and the pressure of economic relations and the interest in economic development more than the environment.[2]

Since 1933 international conventions have slowly developed the legal norms of international environmental law, but after the creation of the UN these norms have been developing progressively and rapidly.[3]

So the treaty law has become the more effective source of international environmental law, since

---

[1] - **ICJ - The Nuclear Tests Cases. (Australia and New Zealand v France).** The ICJ in its Judgment said: (... The duty to refrain from nuclear testing is stated in absolute terms, rather in terms relative to the incidence of the effects of nuclear testing upon particular States. The duty is thus owed to the international community, it is the duty of every State towards every other State. For this reason and - to use the very language of the Court in the Barcelona Tracton Case - because of the importance of the rights involved, all states can be held to have a legal interest in their protection. (ICJ Report 1970. p. 33). Moreover the Court accepted the principle of erga omnes with regard to the fundamental obligations recognized by the international community as a whole and which concern all "humans" (Les obligations, interessant l'ensemble de la communauté internationale et sont absolues dans la mesure où elles resultent de la reconnaissance des droits fondamentaux de toute personne humaine). **Pierre Michel Eisemann, Vincent Coussirat-Coustere Paul Hur. Petit Manuel de La Jurisprudence de La Cour Internationale de Justice.** p. 115.

[2] - **Ilona Cheyne. Environmental Issues in Europe and the Role of International Law.** An article, inter alia, other Articles published in a book entitled **'Green Light on Europe'** edited by Sara Parkin, Heretic Books Ltd. 1991. pp. 286-295. The writer says: "Although the Stockholm Declaration on Human environment was made as long ago as 1972, and despite the projects conducted under the auspices of the UN Environmental Programme, international efforts to discuss and protect the world environment pale in comparison with the time and energy devoted to economic matters. The pressures of international economic relations, and those from domestic, industrial and other interest groups, have dictated that governments have had little choice but to favour economic development over environmental interests. Ibid. p. 289.

[3] - **Alexandre Kiss - Selected Multilateral Treaties in the Field Environment.** UNEP Reference Series 3. Nairobi 1983. In his Foreword the Editor said: "The International legal rules concerning the protection of the environment progress gradually and precedents, even if they do not directly concern a given situation or a given region in the world play an important role." p. VIII.

the early conventions on environment were adopted.[1]

Nowadays there are numerous norms of international environmental law and many of them are global and universal and have the effect of interntional custom.

The role of international organizations in the field of environment has been very effective in developing the characters of these norms especially, in their declarations, resolutions and practices.

One can cite very important environmental universal norms. International organizational norms started their life by declarations and resolutions, and afterwards they developed into custom, when international conferences on environmental law adopt these norms in global mulilateral conventions as treaties, e.g. a catalogue of these norms can be cited.

* The Sovereign rights of the State do not cause environmental damage to another State (Principle 2 of the Stockholm Declaration on Human Environment, 1972).
* The protection of the environment is a universal responsibility of all States (Art. 30 of the Charter of the Rights and Duties of States of 1974).
* The Duty to protect the man and environment against air pollution (Art. 2 of the Convention on Long Range Transboundary Air Pollution of 1979).
* Fair utilization and exploitation of natural resources, they should not be wasted. (Art. 10 of the World Charter for Nature of 1982).
* Nature must be protected against degradation caused by warfare and other hostilities. (Art. 5 of the World Charter for Nature of 1982).
* The Duty to prevent, reduce and control pollution (Art. 194 of the Law of the Sea 1982).
* The Duty of the State to protect, preserve and improve the quality of the environment (EC Single Market Agreement 1984).
* The Polluter should pay compensation for the damage caused to the environment or the victim of pollution (customary norm).
* The Duty of the State to protect the Ozone layer and to cooperate with the international community for this purpose (Art. 2 of the Vienna Convention on the Protection of Ozone Layer 1985).
* The settlement of environmental disputes by peaceful means and if not settled by negotiation, by judicial means and arbitration (customary norm).
* The Declaration of Rio (1992) emphasis on the principle of international consensus regarding the environmental challenges outside the jurisdiction of the (importing) State which concern transboundary or global environment should be met by international consensus.

Besides, there are more than 100 international legal agreements and instruments in force, which involve legal principles and norms that form international environmental custom.[2]

The protection of Mother Earth is a common responsibility of the international community as a whole. Humankind should work together, sharing this responsibility. It is global commons.

---

[1] - See Convention Relative to the Preservation of Fauna and Flora in the Natural State of 8.11.1933. And also The Convention on Nature Protection and Wildlife Preservation in the Western Hemisphere of 12.10.1940. Kiss. Ibid. p. 3.

[2] - UNCED. Guide to Agenda 21. p. 16.

Chapter 2

PROTECTION OF THE ENVIRONMENT

Protection of the environment is the most important subject of international law of the environment. This importance appears in the many international conventions which are in force. Besides, the national legislations of the member-States parties to these conventions which reflect their concern about the protection of the environment. There are three sections in this chapter; the first: **Protection Within the Jurisdiction of the State**, the second: **The Role of International Community**, and the third: **Use of Technology**.

Section 1- Within State's Jurisdiction

Every State within its jurisdiction is responsible about the protection of the environment. This responsibility falls on the burden of the State as the legal person which exercises jurisdiction on its territory which consists of land, sea and air. So the State according to internal and international law is competent for the protection of the environment. This competence involves two obligations: on the one hand, the State is capable for the protection of the territorial environment, and on the other hand, it is responsible for the adoption of a legal order (laws and regulations) and enforcing them on the individuals and other legal persons for the protection of the environment.

A - The State

The State is the effective and competent power within its jurisdiction to protect the environment. It has great authority to do so within its jurisdiction. As the environmental law is growing, the State assumes great power in the development and the enforcement of this law. Every State nowadays, plays a big role in the protection of the environment. The role of the State appears in the numerous domestic legislations at different levels which it and its agencies legislate on different environmental protection issues.

The environmental law enlarged the power and the role of the State in the protection of the environment and the domestic legislations reveal the importance of the role of the State and the many activities which it exercises in the environmental fields. State's role appears in the air, land and sea pollution, safety of food, conservation of nature, protection against and control of the environmental dangers and hazards and the activities which cause pollution and contamination of the environment and the protection of work environment.

When the State exercises its competence regarding the protection of the environment it faces its obligation towards the international community, as the environmental protection concerns the international community as a whole. Thus there must be universal cooperation in the protection of the environment which involves the States and peoples as well as the responsibility of the individuals.

The State exercises a lot of activities in the protection of the environment. These activities have increased under the pressure of the Green movements all over the world. The task of the State, therefore, is not only the protection of the environment and the preservation of nature, habitats and the living resources, but the improvement of the quality of life for all people without discrimination.

Protection of the Environment

There is no doubt that State's protection of the environment which, generally speaking, concerns all States, in the East or the West, or the North or the South, lags behind the need for improving the environmental wellbeing and the quality of life.

Despite the environmental consciousness, many States in the world nowadays lack the means and resources, plans, strategies and legislations which are necessary for the environmental protection.

Even in Europe, where great change took place after the collapse of the Socialist regimes and the democratic trend swept over Eastern Europe, they are feeling the necessity of environmental protection after decades of environmental destruction.

On the other hand, war, internal and civil conflicts in Africa, the Middle East and East Asia have destroyed the environment in many regions of the world. While the State should protect the Environment, we find it or its opponents in war or civil conflicts destroy the environment for the purposes of winning the conflicts. How much destruction and pollution took place in these regions, e.g., the pollution of the gulf region in the Iraqi-Iran war and the Kuwaiti war, especially the burning of the oil wells in Kuwait which polluted the environment in all the region, besides Kuwait.

Therefore the environment protection depends on the capacity of the State and the realization of its strategy for the environmental protection.

Besides, the industrial States face the environmental problems which are caused by the pollution and the contamination of the environment as a result of the consumption of the energy the industry uses. So the State is put under more responsibility to act in order to protect the environment. Thus it is necessary to study the different aspects of the State's role in the protection of the environment. The State role in the environmental protection appears in the legislation which regulates this protection and the enforcement of the law. The environmental role of the State appears in two functions; 1 - the Legislative Function and 2 - the Control, Inspection and Enforcement of the Law and the Environmental Strategy.

1 - The Legislation (Law)

States under pressure of the people consciousness of environmental issues and the demand for care for the environment, became aware of their responsibility for the protection of the environment through legal action by legislating on the environmental issues.

There are many domestic laws on different fields of the States activities on the environment.

It is the State nowadays which exercises the most important role in the protection of the environment, and through the laws, acts and different legislative measures, States use their legislative powers to control, protect the environment or preserve the living habitats or conserve the nature.

Studying the State's legislations in the field of environment necessitates to present a brief study of some important acts in the UK. The points in this study are: a - **Conservation of Nature**, b - **Disposal of Waste**, c - **Human Environment (i. Public Safety, ii. Work Environment, iii. Food and Protection of the Consumers)**, d - **Noise and Nuisance**, e - **Pollution and f - Water.**

a - Conservation of Nature

Conservation of Nature means the preservation, protection and improving the environment and the quality of life. Conservation of nature became an essential function of States nowadays.

Protection of Wildlife

The growing pressure of the Green movements all over the world has had its impact on the State to exercise the function of conservation of mature and the protection of wildlife.

Conservation of nature involves the protection of wildlife, preservation of living resources, animals, plants and natural habitats and the conservation of national culture and heritage. Each of these fields involves great responsibilities on the State and consequently the State legislations in these fields have increased and thus brought about numerous acts and laws.

Besides, the international conventions on nature conservation have added to and increased the involvement of the State in the conservation of nature in addition to its domestic concern.

It is necessary to present in this field UK Acts on the conservation of nature.

i. Protection of Wildlife

The EPA (1990) in the UK is the latest legislation which deals with the protection of wildlife. According to this Act, the NCCS (National Conservation Councils) have been established for England, Wales and Scotland, their responsibilities are the protection of nature and wildlife. And according to Scotland Act (1991), the NCC and the Countryside Commission for Scotland have been merged and a National Heritage Agency has been established.

ii. Preservation of Living Resources

This is a broad subject, where the State is required to adopt a well planned policy and strategy for the protection of living resources. The preservation of living resources involves the protection of fauna and flora which are subject to international protection by several international conventions, the protection of endangered species, the protection of animals, plants, fisheries and marine resources. The preservation of living resources in the UK comes under several Acts e.g. National Parks and Access to Countryside Act 1949, Protection of Birds Act 1954, Water Resources Act 1963 and 1991, Conservation of Seals Act 1970, Wildlife and Countryside Acts 1981 and 1985, Food and Environment Protection Act 1985, EPA 1990 and Wildlife Conservation Act (Fisheries) 1992.

The strategy of the preservation of living resources aims at achieving a natural life cycle of the living resources and ensuring the protection of species and the preservation of food stocks.

iii. Protection of Wild Birds

Section 1 of Part (1) of Wildlife and Countryside Act (1981) provides for the protection of wild birds, the nests, eggs, it incriminates everyone who commits an office if:

1. kills, injures or takes any wild birds;
2. takes, damages or destroys the nest of any wild bird while that nest is in use or being built, or;
3. takes or destroys an egg of any wild bird.

The Act exempts from the ambit of the previous Section if the person is authorized by a licence to catch or hunt outside the forbidden season.

Thus the protection is enforced during the forbidden season of hunting and catching where the birds generate and hive.

iv. Other Animals

Part 1 of the Wildlife and Countryside Act (1981) also protects other animals of different species, fish and specially endangered species.

v. Plants

The Act protects wild plants and rare plants where it prohibits to pick, uproot or destroy any

Protection of the Environment

plant enlisted in Schedule 8 of the Act[1].

vi. Habitat

The habitats are the natural living spaces of plants and other animal species. The environmental law is the important legal instrument for the protection of habitats in the domestic jurisdiction of the State. Both international and national law agree on the protection of habitats. The protection of habitats is a very broad subject, because it deals with domestic and international jurisdiction. The first entitles the State to protect within its legal system and by the adoption of national laws which every State legislates, and so far as it concerns this subject, it is difficult to refer to all legislations of every State in this topic, as the book will become an encyclopedia or a large directory.

But as the habitats are a very important subject in the book, so it is necessary to deal with under the UK law. There are some Acts that deal with habitats, e.g. National Parks and Access to the Countryside Act (1949), Wildlife and Countryside Act (1981), Nature Conservation Act (1984), EPA (1990) and Wildlife Conservation Act - Fisheries (1992), and other legislative instruments[2] concerning the protection of habitats of certain animals and plants.

There are several Fisheries Acts, concerning the protection of Seal, Whale and Salmon in certain periods, areas and mode of catching.[3]

These Acts either establish institutions, local committees to control or enforce the Acts, e.g. NNR, SSSI and LFC or empower the Secretary of State to take or to approve certain decisions taken by the designated authority.

Another aspect of improving the habitats is the care for parks and the beauty of nature.

The National Parks and Access to Countryside Act (1949) in the UK[4] establishes the National Park Commission (NPC) whose duty is exercising of the functions:

Part 1, Section 1(a) Preservation and enhancement or improvements of parks as areas of natural beauty.

(b) encouraging the provision of improvement, for persons resorting to national parks, of facilities for the enjoyment thereof and for the enjoyment of the opportunities for open-air recreation and study of nature afforded thereby.

This Act in Part 2 creates National Parks in order to enhance the natural beauty and open-air recreation. It gives the meaning of Nature Reserve (NR) which the Act provides under suitable conditions and control for special opportunities for study and research into matters relating to the fauna and flora of Great Britain of the physical conditions in which they live and for the study of geological and physiological features of special interest in the area.

Moreover, this Act has two advantages: the creation of NR and the Sites of special scientific interest SSSI.[5]

The SSSI is a place chosen for its special interest to scientists so that it may have an important scientific value for the habitats and the protection of wildlife.

---

[1] - Halibury Statutes No. 32 (Wildlife and Countryside Act (1981)). Butterworths. Ball and Bell. Ibid. p. 348.

[2] - Also Fisheries Act (1981), Salmon & Freshwater Fisheries Act (1975). Halisburys No. 18

[3] - Seal Fisheries (North Pacific) Act (1895 and 1912), Whaling Industry (Regulations) Act (1934). Sea Fish Industry Act (1938), Conservation of Seal Act (1970) and Salmon and Freshwater Fisheries Act (1975).

[4] - See details of the Act in Halisbury's Statutes (32). Butterworths 1987

[5] - Ibid. Part 2.

Disposal of Waste

b - Disposal of Waste

Waste as the ECJ defined in (Vesseso v Zenitti) cases 206-207/88 is any refused material which causes potential health 'hazards' without taking into account their value as recyclable raw materials[1] the ordinary meaning of waste is rubbish.[2] But the EPA (1990) gives different definitions in S. 75(2) of the Act.

S.75(2) 'Waste' includes-

(a) any substance which constitutes a scrap material or any effluent or other unwanted surplus substance arising from the application of any process and

(b) any substance or article which required to be disposed of as being broken, worn out, contaminated or otherwise spoiled;

but does not include a substance which is an explosive within the meaning of Explosive Act of 1875.

(3) Anything which is discarded or otherwise dealt with as it were waste shall be presumed to be waste unless the contrary is proved.

Moreover, Para. (4) of this Section defines 'Controlled Waste' as household, industrial and commercial waste or any such waste.[3]

The duty of the State nowadays involves the protection of the environment from dangerous wastes which cause hazards, sickness and create environmental pollution.

Since the earliest civilization, thinkers and philosophers had given beautiful pictures of a beautiful city which is clean of waste which is harmful to health.

Among the great philosophers who had dealt with this problem was Aristotle who wrote in his (Politics)[4] that the rulers have an obligation towards their citizens to care for the environment and its security, especially, about eternal goods which bring happiness to the individuals,[5] e.g. he referred to the beauty of the city and the necessity of making pools, springs and the construction of large reservoirs of rain water which is necessary for the citizens and the necessity of care for the health of citizens and this he believed depends on a clean environment where it must be a place being well situated on healthy ground with clean water supplies clean of waste.[6]

Waste has advantages and disadvantages, its advantage in an industrial city is that it can be used for economic benefits, by recycling and thus it creates new goods less costly. And if so, it must not be left in a place which creates danger and hazard to the public health and safety, if it were a hazardous waste.

And its disadvantages is that it creates hazards to the public health and safety. So it must be put under control and therefore, it needs good management to save the environment from contamination and pollution.

The EPA has classified the "controlled waste" into household, commercial, industrial and special waste.

In this classification the Act took into account the source which contributes to the waste.

---

[1] - LMELR (1990-2). **Simon Ball & Stuart Bell - Environmental Law**. Blackstone Press 1991, p. 268

[2] - **Green Dictionary, Colin Johnson**. Optima Book 1991.

[3] - See Paras. 5, 6 and 7 of this Section which explain the different kinds of 'Controlled Waste'.

[4] - **Aristotle. Politics.** Translated by H. Rackham. William Heineman and Harvard University Press. 1967 Ed. pp. 553, 583-589.

[5] - Ibid.

[6] - Ibid.

Protection of the Environment

In cities and industrial centres the waste is increasing year after year, and so there are millions of tonnes of rubbish and refuse which cost large sums of money spent on the disposal of waste, from households, people's properties and industrial centres. This waste can be recycled and therefore, it can produce valuable materials and goods and regenerate the environment.

So taking recycling into account, the waste can be classified into useful waste; waste that can be recycled and creates useful materials and dangerous waste which creates hazards; it is harmful to health and public safety.

The most dangerous waste is the nuclear waste.[1] The nuclear waste can be dangerous for a long time. It is produced by several nuclear processes, the nuclear fission, and becomes radioactive waste which is very dangerous to human life and the environment. Also the nuclear power stations, nuclear power industry and even X-rays hospitals create nuclear waste which is unlike ordinary rubbish and is very dangerous to the environment and people.[2]

On the other hand it is necessary to dispose of the nuclear waste in safe places and not to dump it into the sea or in land where it causes constant radiation and therefore leads to the contamination of the environment, whether the soil, the air or by the radiation which creates diseases harmful to the public health and safety.

As waste affects the environment and has large dimensions, so it is valuable to study the waste management under the UK law.

i. Waste Management in the UK

The latest Act in the UK which deals with waste is the (1990) Act on the Environmental Protection (EPA).

ii. Meaning of Waste

The Act in S. 75(1-2) has given different meanings of waste as quoted in p. 22 as scrap, spoiled or unwanted materials.

Paras. 5, 6 and 7 of this Section define the different kinds of 'controlled waste' mentioned under Para. 4.

While Para. 8 specified 'Special Waste' as another kind of 'controlled waste', it does not define it but left it to be defined by special regulations, any how, special waste is subject to be controlled in each case as it is hazardous and dangerous.[3]

On the other hand there are some judgements of courts which deal with waste.[4]

---

[1] - **Despite the advantages of waste management, but still waste disposal needs more enlightened methods.** Struan Simpson. The Times Guides to the Environment. 1990. p 792.

[2] - Jem Eldridge. Save our Planet. Magnet Book 1987. pp. 72-73

[3] - DOE. Ibid.

[4] - The ECJ in its judgment in the case of Vessoso v Zanetti 206-207/88, 2 LMELR 133 (1990) said, that the definition of waste was properly concerned with potential health hazards that the material could bring. The Court did not take into account the usefulness of the material to be recycled.

In another case, Rotherham Metropolitan Borough Council, ex parte Rankin JEL 251 (1990), the Court said that the term (waste) should be given its ordinary meaning... and that the treatment and recycling of solvents could amount to the treatment of waste.

In Kent County Council v Queenborough Rolling Mill Co Ltd JEL 257 ((1990) the Court said that the important factor was the nature of the material when it was discarded. **Simon Ball and Stuart Bell.** Ibid. pp. 267 - 268

Waste Management in U.K.

iii. Control of Waste

Both COPA (Control of Pollution Act) 1974 and EPA 1990 regulate the control of waste. Besides the UN Convention on the Control of transboundary of Hazardous Wastes (Basel, 22.3.82).[1]

The COPA provided for adequate system for the disposal of waste in order to protect the environment and created local authorities for the control of waste.

The main task of local authorities is to put local plan which should contain 'sites' and 'specific policies' for the disposal of waste.[2]

The EPA (1990) has introduced some changes on the control of disposal of waste, but it maintained the system under COPA (1974).[3] Although waste management and control are largely a business of local housekeeping, they are essentially a central and major issue, in that waste affects the State and its international obligations and so it has an international effect, especially, the protection of global enviroment and the international trade of waste.[4]

The increase of waste in industrial countries necessitates the drawing up of a policy on waste management and control, in order to clean the environment from waste, if at least the efforts to decrease the waste do not succeed.

It is said that the best policy of combating waste is the application of the four (R) verbs: repair, re-use, recycle and reduce waste.[5]

The disposal of waste is a very important problem in the protection of environment, so nobody can minimize the role of the State in the disposal of waste, whether it creates hazards or can be used economically in recycling, industrial development or international trade.

For these reasons the waste system in the developed countries, the US and Japan has been considered as very important, in order to protect the environment on one hand and the duty of care in the disposal of waste on the other hand.

In the UK the disposal of waste system has been planned to achieve five aims. The first is that the protection of the environment necessitates to cleanse it from the waste, and the second; is the necessity of recycling and waste generates energy, the third; is the tight control over waste disposal, the fourth; is the collection of litter (rubbish) from door to door and forbidding dumping it in the streets and the fifth; is the international responsibility concerning the environment.[6]

Concerning the first point the main Acts which have set up the waste system are: the COPA (1974), Town and Country Planning Act (Hazardous Substances) 1990, EPA 1990, and Town and Country (Compensation) Act 1991.

These Acts have drawn up local measures for the management and control of waste as it has a strong impact on the environment and its effects on the economy and public health and safety.

---

[1] - The UN Convention on the Control of Transboundary Movements of Hazardous Wastes and their Disposal signed in Basel on 22.3.89, defines waste (Art. 3) as substances which are disposed of or are intended to be disposed of or are required to be disposed of by the provisions of National Law. Under Annex (3) of the Convention there is classification of waste, inter alia, Annex (2) both mention Waste categories e.g. Waste having as constituents requiring special considerations or other kinds of waste enlisted which have hazardous characteristics which are explosive, flammable solids, flammable liquids or substances which generate oxygen that contributes to combustion.

[2] - Ibid. pp. 264-265.
[3] - Department of the Environment (DOE). Waste Management and Recycling.
[4] - The Times Guide to the Enviroment. Ibid. p. 79.
[5] - **Paul Harrison. The Third Revolution.** Taurus & Co Ltd and Worldwide for Nature. 1992. p 194.
[6] - DOE. Ibid

Protection of the Environment

The new legal development introduced by the EPA is that it made some changes on waste disposal, the powers of the local authorities (Waste Regulation Authorities WRA), the local Waste Disposal Authorities Contractors (LWDAC), the responsibility arising from waste disposal, as the EPA puts the responsibility on the authority which disposes of waste.

The law now puts the responsibility on whom handles the waste, because, has a duty of care towards the victim individually, or the community as a whole regarding the public health and safety.

Moreover, the Act penalizes the individual who disposes litter (rubbish), Part IV of the Act, if commits an offence and be responsible to clear it, or others who fail to clear the waste and confers powers on the local authority to take legal measures against the offender and to fine him or her (maximum £2,500).

The purpose of this Act is to make the roads and streets clear of waste and be kept clean. The law sets a code of practice on the cleanliness.[1]

iv. Waste Authorities

The EPA grants powers to local authorities to manage and dispose of waste. The DOE calls these authorities Duty Bodies,[2] which according to the Act consist of two kinds of bodies, the WRAs and LWDACs. The first are local authorities, they are district authorities formed on the basis of county or metropolitan framework.

In the circulars issued by the County Councils, e.g. the Surrey County Council in its pamphlet on (Surrey Caring for the Environment) says: "the Council will protect the environment by:-
. Reducing air, land and waste pollution:
* Discouraging waste and encouraging the conservation and recycling of waste resources.

The Environmental Audit Working Group (EAWG) founded by the Council is to co-ordinate with Green Teams established by each department in order to address the environmental issues of each area.[3]

While (LWDACs) are private companies, or joint ventures formed by both private company and waste disposal authority, whose task to act as waste collection authority provided by S. 45 of EPA.[4]

The powers of Waste Regulating Authorities (WRAs) involve setting of policies, planning of

---

[1] - DOE. Waste Management and Recycling. The duty of each Waste Collection Authority to arrange collection of waste. S. 48. The duty of Waste Collection Authority to deliver the disposal of waste collected to a place as the waste disposal authority directs (EPA)Ibid.

[2] - DOE. Leaflet on Litter and the Law. Justice Hobhouse in Regina v Avon County Council, Export Terry Adams Ltd (Court of Appeal - judgement of 16 January 1994) said that there were undoubted difficulties for local authorities under Part II of EPA (1990) as a result in combination of the three statutory objectives which were liable to conflict with each other. The judge mentioned these objectives as:
(1) Objective which related to the environment considerations which arose from the disposal of waste of and the requirement that a local authority regard to the considerations.
(2) Second objective was the local authorities should divest themselves of so much of their undertakings as related to the disposal, keeping, treatment and collection of waste.
(3) Third objectives. Was the disposal of waste should be the subject of an open competition.... to make full use of skills and facilities available on the open market. The Times Law Report 20.1.94. This judicial opinion expresses the importance of Waste disposal in the environmental considerations.

[3] - See 'Surrey Caring for our Environment. Surrey County Council 3/93. Also, Hounslow Recycling Guide 1993 calls for Reduction of Waste, p. 6.

[4] - S. 45 Collection of Controlled Waste.

Waste Authorities

waste disposal which include environmental control, collection, recycling and licensing of waste disposal.

Ss. 51, 52(1) and 55 of EPA provide that WRAs must arrange the disposal of controlled waste, recycling and licensing. The Waste Regulating Authorities (WRAs) must put recycling plan.[1] But all local councils have now great powers to run recycling schemes.[2]

The disposal of waste is nowadays a great issue on a worldwide level, especially the special 'hazardous waste' which includes radioactive and chemical waste which needs control as it is dangerous to life and public health.

The most dangerous is the radioactive and nuclear waste. Nuclear power stations produce dangerous materials, when the spent (used fuels rods) are taken out of the reactor.

All nuclear waste needs to be safely stored for a long time, as far as the radioactivity is alive and this continues for not hundreds, but thousands, of years.[3]

Great amounts of individual wastes are buried and disposed of in landfills where they are sites in which waste is disposed of in large quantities. 80% of all waste in the UK is disposed of in landfills.[4] Approximately four million tonnes, the industrial waste is disposed of in these landfills.[5] While incineration (burning) accounts for 10% of it.[6]

There is much criticism about the lack of control on waste disposal in landfills, where dangerous materials and chemicals need treatment and control.[7]

While DoE says that care and control are adequate to protect the environment from the dangerous waste dumped in these landfills.[8]

Landfill gas causes great hazard to the environment, which can be well managed by producing a great resources by good management.[9]

v. Licences

The concept of waste licences is derived from the need of waste control, the protection of the environment and public health and safety.

The EPA widens the control and tightens the control of waste, S.33 of the Act provides:

It makes an offence:

(a) to deposit controlled waste or knowingly cause or knowingly permit controlled waste to be deposited in or on land unless there is a waste management licence in force and the deposit is in accordance with it;

(b) to treat, keep or dispose of controlled waste, or knowingly cause or knowingly permit controlled waste to be treated, kept or disposed of in or on land by means of mobile plant except

---

[1] - DOE. Waste Management and Recycling. Ibid.
[2] - Ibid.
[3] - Nigel **Hawkes**. Nuclear Safety. Franklin Wats 1986. p. 25
[4] - DOE. Ibid, while other sources says the percentage is 90%. British Steel. Can Recycling. Recyclobedia. Steel Can Recycling Information Bureau. 93. p. 18.
[5] - **Angella Snyth and Caroline Wheate. The Green Guide.** Argus Books 1990. p 84
[6] - British Steel. Recyclobedia. Ibid.
[7] - **A Snyth and C Wheate.** Ibid.
[8] - DoE. Ibid. British Steel. Ibid.
[9] - British Steel Recyclobedia. Ibid. p 19. The figures disclosed in the EEC show that the Community generates 2 billion tonnes of waste annually, of it 150m tonnes industrial waste and between 20-30m tonnes of hazardous waste. Environmental Policy in the EC, p. 35. Imagine how much damage this waste does to the environment. And so the need of good waste management and recycling is necessary.

Protection of the Environment

where a waste management licence is in force;
(c) to treat, keep or dispose of controlled waste in a manner likely to cause pollution of the enviroment or harm human health.

S.35 (12) of EPA defines waste licence, it means a 'waste management licence', 'site licence' and 'mobile plant licence' mean, respectively, a licence authorising the treatment, keeping or disposal of waste in or on land and a licence authorising the treatment, or disposal of waste by means of mobile plant.

The 'Waste Regulation Authority' grants the licence to the occupier of the land where the waste is treated or the person who operates the plant concerning 'waste mobile plant'.

S.35(3) of the Act involves the conditions and terms of granting the licence relating to the activities and precautions to be taken at works carried out.

S.35(6) of the same Act grants the Secretary of State powers. He may make regulations concerning the conditions provided in Para (3) of the same Section in different circumstances. According to S.35(7) of the same Section the Secretary of State may give directions to the 'waste regulations authority' about the terms and conditions of granting the licence.

S.37 authorises the WRA to modify the licence while in force, also the holder of the licence can apply to the WRA to modify the licence.

The purpose of the WRA according to Para. (2) of this Section is the protection of the environment and that the authorised activities do not harm the public health or become seriously detrimental to the amenities and locality affected by these activities.

Para. (3) of the same Section authorises the Secretary of State to give directions to the WRA about the modifications of the conditions of the licence. The directions are binding on the WRA.

S.38 of EPA allows the WRA to revoke the licence which is in force, if the conditions under Paras. a, b and c of this Section are met, that the holder of the licence is unfit for reason of being convicted of relevant offence, or his activities would cause pollution or harm health or cause threat to the amenities of the locality and that the modification of the licence cannot avoid the pollution and the harm to the locality.

Para. (2) of the same Section authorises the WRA also to revoke the licence in case of activities authorised ceased to be in the hands of the technically competent person.

If the licence were revoked, it should cease to have effect (Para 5).

Para (6) of the same Section authorises the WRA to suspend the licence in respect of the activities authorised by the licence wholly or partly as it specifies in suspending the licence.

vi. Civil Liability for Damage

The duty of care for the disposal of waste by the person who produces, transfers or deposits in any place which causes harm or damage to the individual, the environment, the public health and safety, is strictly imposed by the law nowadays, besides the criminal responsibility, if the action would constitute an offence according to the law.

The person responsible about the waste is under civil liability to compensate the victim of the damage or harm.

vii. Council of Europe Convention on Civil Liability

The principles of civil liability for damage caused by waste have been recently codified by the

Council of Europe Convention on Civil Liability

recent Council of Europe Convention signed on 21.6.93 in Lugano.[1] This Convention has been adopted by the EEC and the Members of the Council of Europe and is open to other States which are non-members of both organisations.

(a) Main Principles

The main principles of this Convention are:-
Liability of the operator in respect of dangerous substances, organism and certain waste installations or sites as provided in Art. 6:-

1. The operator in respect of dangerous activity mentioned under Art. 2, Para. 1, Sub-paras. (a to c) shall be liable for the damage caused by the activity as a result of incidents at the time or during the period when he was exercising the control of that activity.

2. If an incident of a continuous occurrence, all the operators successfully exercising the control of the dangerous activity during that occurrence shall be jointly and severally liable. However, the operator who proves that the occurrence during the period when he was exercising the control of the dangerous activity caused only a part of the damage shall be liable for that part of the damage only.

Para. 3 of this Article puts the liability on the operator at the time of the occurrence if he exercises the control of the waste partly when he proves that he is liable for that part of damage only.

While Para. 4 of this Article puts the liability on the last operator of the dangerous activity if the damage becomes known after the dangerous activity ceased, unless that operator proves that he was not liable for the damage at the time of his operation or the waste activity. If it is proved, the previous Paras. of this Article are applicable.

While Art. 7 deals with liability in resepct of sites for the permanent deposit of waste, it provides:-

(b) Total & Partial Liability and Disputes Between Operators

1. The operator of a site for the permanent deposit of waste at the time when damage caused by waste deposited at that site becomes known shall be liable for this damage. Should the damage caused by waste deposited before the closure of such a site known after that closure, the last operator shall be liable.

2. Liability under this Article shall apply to the exclusion of any liability of the operator under Article 6 irrespective of the nature of the waste.

3. Liability under this Article shall apply to the exclusion of any liability of the operator under Article 6 if the same operator conducts another dangerous activity on the site for the permanent deposit of waste.

However, if the operator or the person who has suffered damage proves that only a part of the damage was caused by the activity concerning the permanent deposite of waste, this Article shall only apply to that part of the damage.

4. Nothing in this Convention shall produce any right of recourse of the operator against any third party.

(c) Exemption from Liability

The Convention exempts the operator from liability under Art. 8 in the following conditions:
The operator shall not be liable under this Convention for damage which he proves:

---

[1] - On Civil Liability for Damage Resulting from Activity Dangerous to the Environment. There is also the International Convention of Transboundary Movements of Hazardous Wastes of Basel (April 1991) which sets up the principles of liability and compensation.

Protection of the Environment

1. was caused by an act of war, hostilities, civil war, insurrection or a natural phenomenon of an exceptional, inevitable and irresistible character;
2. was caused by an act done with the intent to cause damage by a third party, despite safety measures appropriate to the type of dangerous activity in question;
3. resulted necessarily from compliance with a specific order or compulsory measures of a public authority;
4. was caused by pollution at tolerable levels under local relevant circumstances; or
5. was caused by a dangerous activity taken lawfully in the interests of the person who suffered the damage, whereby it was reasonable towards this person to expose him to the risks of the dangerous activity.

It is noticed that the Convention does not apply to the damge arising from carriage. The carriage in this Article includes the period from which the beginning of the process of loading until the end of the process of unloading. However the Convention shall apply to carriage by pipeline, as well as to carriage performed entirely in an installation or on a site unaccessible to the public where it is an accessory to other activities and is an integral part thereof.

Also the Convention does not apply to damage caused by a nuclear substance (Art. 4/2). The nuclear incident liability is regulated by the Paris Convention of 29 July 1960 and its Supplementary Convention of Brussels of 31 January 1963 or the Vienna Convention of 21 May 1963 on Civil liability for Nuclear Damage; or as the CoE Convention provides, if the liability is regulated by a specific internal law which is more favourable, with regard to compensation of damage, taking into account any instrument referred to in the previous sub-paragraph a.

The Convention as provided in Art. 4/3 should not be applicable where it contradicts the rules of the applicable law concerning the compensation of workers or social security scheme.

(d) The Convention applies to damage after its enforcement

Regarding the occurrence of a series of incidents, beginning before the entry of the Convention into force, only the incidents which occur after the enforcement of the Convention are regarded subject to the Convention, where the liability for the damage can be brought in legal proceedings before the courts, where the plaintiff can ask for compensation for the damage caused by the waste.

The Convention, according to Art. 5 regards the last operator is liable for the damage, when it is known, provided that it was resulted from a dangerous activity even if the installation or site ceased to exist, if the damage occurred after the Convention came into force and so the defender can prove that damage occurred in a time he was not the operator, he can deny partly or totally his liability, the incident had occurred before the Convention came into force or the incident had occurred at a time when another operator was responsible for the damage, Art 6(4).

It appears from the Convention that the liability of the damage resulting from the waste disposal rests on the operator at the time of the incident that takes place (Art. 6).

(e) Recourse against the Third Party

The Convention grants the operator the right of recourse against a third party if the latter is liable for the damage (Art. 6/5).

(f) Compensation

Art. 2/7 of the Convention defines the damage as:-
1. - loss of life or personal injury
2. - loss or damage to property other than to the installation itself or property held under the control of the operator, at the site of the dangerous activity.
3. - loss or damage by impairment of the environment in so far as this is not considered to be

damage within the meaning of sub-paragraphs a or b above provided that compensation for the impairment of the environment, other than for loss of profit from such impairment, shall be limited to the costs of measures of reinstatement actually undertaken or to be undertaken.

4. - the costs of preventive measures and any loss caused by preventive measures, to the extent that the loss of damage referred to in sub-paragraphs a to c of this Paragraph arises out of, or results from, the hazardous properties of the dangerous substances, genetically modified organisms or micro-organisms or arises or results from waste.

The Convention defines (**Measures of reinstatement**) for the purpose of compensation in Art. 2/8, as any reasonable measures aiming to reinstate or restore damaged components of the environment, or to introduce, where reasonable, the equivalent of these components into the environment. Internal law may indicate who will be entitled to take such measures.

While '**Preventive Measures**' according to the Convention (Art. 2/9) are any reasonable measures taken by any person, after an incident has occurred to prevent or minimise loss or damage as referred to in para. 7, sub-paras a to c of this Article.

It appears from this Convention that the compensation of the damage is left to national law and the domestic courts of the Parties.

This is clear from Art. 19 on Jurisdiction which provides:-
1. where the damage was suffered;
2. where the dangerous activity was conducted; or
3. where the defendant has his habitual residence.

While the criteria of compensation are decided by the court according to national law, the common law in the UK or the civil law in other Member-States or other special or particular laws which govern the compensation of damage or injury.

The court, however, exercises large discretion in deciding the compensation which covers the loss of life, injury or loss of property, loss of profit or economic loss in cases of individual claims.

There is no difficulty in considering the compensation in such cases. But the case may be complicated in concern the compensation of impairment to the environment or public utility. It seems from Art. 2(7c) of the Convention that it minimises the extent of compensation by the costs of measures of reinstatement actually undertaken or to be undertaken provided that the loss of profit from such impairment is not governed by this Article and subject to the general rules of compensation that govern the case.

(g) Jurisdiction

The Convention, according to Art. 19 confers jurisdiction on the court of place to decide waste disputes, where the damage was suffered, or the dangerous activity was conducted or where the defendant has his ordinary residence. These matters are decided according to the general principles of private international law or the conflict of laws. Nevertheless the court applies lex fori in such matters as far as the Convention cannot determine all kinds of disputes in advance.

(h) Time Bar

The Convention, according to Art. 17 limits the time bar for action by three years from the date on which the claimant knew or ought reasonably to have known of the damage and the identity of the operator.

The Convention refers to the laws of Parties regulating the suspension, and interruption of limitation periods in determining the limitation of period (Art. 17(1)).

In the case of continuous occurrence and a series of incidents, the Convention limits the period by 30 years which begins from the date of the last incident which caused the damage. In respect of a site for the permanent deposit of waste the thirty years period runs at the latest from the date on which the site was closed according to the provisions of internal law Art. 17(2).

viii. Recycling and Planning

Recycling and planning of waste disposal are important issues in the protection of the environment. The Wildlife and Countrysides Act (1981), Town and Country Planning Act (1990) and Compensation Act (1991) have granted the local authorities the power to initiate policies which involve local development plans for waste disposal and recycling (TCPA-1990, S.36).

The DoE has proposal addressed to County Authorities to prepare disposal development plans. While S. 38 of PCA (Planning and Compensation Act) defined waste policies as development plans in respect of disposal of refuse or waste materials other than mineral waste.

The same Section has defined "Waste Local Plans" as plans containing waste policies.

So the local development plans, according to these two Acts involve the strategy of waste disposal, the areas of disposal and recycling plans.

The importance of recycling plans is that they reflect the great environmental consciousness about the use of waste materials which need wide areas of land to dump in, but instead of that they can be recycled and produce economically many useful products. This is beneficial substitution to raw materials which could cause consumption of environmental resource, if there had not been recycling.

So recycling is a great industrial development of waste and the protection of environment from waste pollution and the preservation of natural resources from consumption and a sound way of economy by recycling the waste instead of raw materials which would cost more than the waste which is cheap or would cost much if were dumped in addition to the harm which is caused to the environment.

Recycling development planning is a great and successful policy of the preservation of natural resources, keeping the balance of ecology system. It has become global strategy in the protection of the environment and the prevention of pollution.

Moreover the industrial countries are now using advanced technology in the eco-development of waste and recycling.

This strategy is very effective now, in many products which are sold in markets nowadays at low prices, cheaper than the price of goods produced from raw materials.

This demonstrates the economies of recycling. Here in the UK there are many private enterprises, industrial firms, corporations and chains of supermarkets which are recycling waste and contributing to the protection of the environment and the implementation of green policy.

The countries of the EEC, as a result of the Directives on the environment are implementing them including these which concern recycling and waste disposal.

Despite Art. 130r under Title XVI on the Environment, there is silence about waste management, it did not grant the Council any power to take action concerning the waste management. It seems from this Article that it has let the EEC to follow its objectives for the protection of the environment in general terms.[1]

---

[1] - See **Maastricht Treaty**. Art 130r(2), this policy has stressed the precautionary and preventive principles of the environmental policy of the European Community. This provision based on the subsidiarity which is left to the national authorities to decide.

Recycling saves energy, besides its protective benefits in producing recycled materials.[1] And this saves the environment from warming. Nowadays great enterprises, firms and establishments have their own schemes for recycling. Among these are supermarkets, food chains, British Steel and National Westminster Bank.[2]

Recycling of waste materials in many countries is growing. In Germany steel can recycling amounts to 50% of the steel can packaging.[3]

In the US, the Federal Government estimates the recycling of 25% of waste materials. Also the recycling of Aluminium is about 75% of cans.[4]

c - **Human Environment (i. Public Safety and Health, ii. Work Environment, iii. Food and Protection of the Consumers)**

Human environment is the most important topic of environmental study, because man is the subject and object of human environment. He is the subject, because, he affects the environment he lives in, an object, because the environment affects him.

So there is great action and reaction between man and the environment. The object of human environment is to improve the quality of life, to put enough environmental resources at his disposal and to ensure his chance to work and to prosper, to have a good house to live in, a good climate for his leisure time to enjoy.

The environmental movement since it began, its purposes were to sustain the human living and to improve the quality of life and the protection of the environment, which gives food, resources and energy to man in order to live and develop the resources of the environment. Art. 130r of the Treaty of Maastricht provides that the policy of the environment should be, as concerns the citizens of the Community is the protection of their health and the economic and social development of the Community and the balanced development of its regions. This policy indicates that the improvement of the human environment should go hand in hand with development. Thus human environment stands on public safety and health, protection of work environment (place of work), food, products liability and the protection of consumers.

These are the fundamental responsibility of the State in order to fulfill its function as concerns the environment.

The Stockholm principles adopted by the UN Conference on Human Environment (16 June 1972) in Stockholm stressed in its preamble (Para. 2) that the protection and improvement of the human environment is a major issue which affects the well-being of peoples and economic

---

[1] - The energy needed for the production of one aluminium can, can produce 20 recycled ones. Tesco's pamphlet on Creen Choice. Global warming and Ozone Depletion.

[2] - National Westminster Bank is one of the leading British Companies playing its part. It has done so in a systematic and committed way through its environmental responsibilities, set up in the eighties. The NatWest also joined the UN Support Group of Banks on the protection and improvement of the Environment. NatWest Environment Review. 1993. pp. 1 and 7.

[3] - **British Steel.** Steel Can Recycling Information Bureau. Domestic Waste Recycling - Meeting the Challenge 93. p. 77. Also France has achieved great level of steel recovery from Waste. Ibid. The British Steel has successful scheme for recycling steel for the production of cans for packaging. It appears from this publication that the British Steel has very well dealt with recycling economy. Recycling is also growing in paper, aluminium, plastic, glass and food and drinks industries.

[4] - **British Steel Recyclobedia.** Ibid. p. 88. The Environment Secretary made written orders to newspapers and industry executives to increse the use and production from non-recycled waste and to increase recycling of 40% by the year 2000. The Independent newspaper said it used 30% of recycled paper. The Independent, 8.11.93.

Protection of the Environment

development throughout the world; it is the urgent desire of the peoples of the whole world and the duty of all Governments.

Thus the Declaration calls upon all States to co-operate and fulfill their obligations towards their peoples and to improve the human environment.

The human being is the fundamental factor who affects the environment as can improve and change it in limits, and by his/her many effective activities can create great changes and developments of the environment which took place through centuries.

On the other hand, he/she was and still is the slave of his environment, as nature by its formidable forces inflicted, and still is inflicting, great dangers, damages and threats to humankind.

Dealing with human environment necessitates to study the State's legislation in the following points:-

i. Public Safety and Health

Public Safety involves the protection of citizens from environmental dangers and hazards and fighting epidemic diseases which cause threat to their lives and the protection of their health. So public safety involves also public health.

The State's activities and services in the field of public safety and health are enormous. There are many laws and legislations which cover wide variety of State's activities and services in the field of public safety and health.[1]

In the UK the Acts which deal with this field are: the Control of Pollution Acts (1974, 1989), EPA (1990), Public Health Act (1961), Radio-active Substances Act (1961), Rivers Pollution, - Protection and Prevention Acts (1951, 1961), Town and Country Planning Acts (1965, 1971, 1990) and Water Act (1989).

So the State activities in the field of public safety are increasing, because environmental dangers and hazards cause great threats to the public safety as pollution[2] (air, land and water), epidemic diseases, waste[3] and atmospheric hazards need constant watch, in order that the State can protect the public. So the functions of the State nowadays become very wide and important in order to protect public health and safety.

Even private enterprises and individuals are required by law to prevent risks which cause threat to the public health and safety. In Regina V, the Board of Trustees of the Science Museum, The Court of Appeal said in its judgment on 15.3.92 that Section 3 of the Health and Safety at Work Act (1974) provides' (1) It shall be the duty of every employer to conduct his undertaking in such a way as to ensure, so far as is reasonably practicable, that persons not in his employment who may be affected thereby are not exposed to risks to their health or safety'. And where an

---

[1] - The Court of Appeal said in its judgement of 23 September 1993 in (Adams v Southern Electricity Board) the Southern Electricity owed a duty of care for intelligent teenager to ensure that he was effectively prevented from climbing up a pole mounted high voltage electrical installation. The Board was in breach of its duty at Common Law to fix and maintain effective anti-climbing devices. The Times, October 1993.

[2] - See Clear Air Act (1968) Part (1) Air Pollution control and pollution and emission of gasses which pollute the air and harm public health/ and S. 106 of EPA.... 'Preventing and minimising any damage which may arise from the escape or release from human control of genetically modified organisms.'

[3] - The Action of Greenpeace v British Nuclear Fuel (BNFL) Thorp Nuclear Processing Plant at Sellafield, Cumbria which objected to the Action on the assumption that Greenpeace had no locus standi. The Court (HC) said that Greenpeace had locus standi, but the public health and safety were properly taken into account. The Times Law Report on 30.9.93. Also the HC dismissed the Action of Gateshead Council V. Environment Secretary concerning the clinical waste incinerator at Wardley, Tyne and Wear and allowed the Scheme as there is no danger to the environment. Ibid.

Work Environment

employee was charged under Section 3(1) of the Health and Safety at Work Act 1974 with exposing members of the public to risks to their health from exposure to legionella pneumophila, the prosecution need not show that members of the public had actually inhaled the bacterium or that it had been there to be inhaled, it was sufficient to show that there had been a risk of it being there'[1]

But the High Court in its judgment on 8.10.93 in the Action of Elizabeth Reag v British Nuclear Fuels Ltd (BNFL) and Vivien Hope v (BNFL), said the cases were unsupported scientifically and there was no evidence that the project at Sellafield causes leukaemia to children.[2]

ii. **Work Environment**

The Maastricht Treaty under 'Social Policy' ... "Title VIII" provided in Art. 8a(1) that Member-States shall pay particular attention to encouraging improvements, especially in the <u>Work Environment</u>

So, what is meant by work environment?

Work environment is a broad and complicated term, it involves several areas of application in that it involves:-

(a) Health and safety at work;
(b) Social conditions of work;
(c) Control and protection of working conditions and from hazardous substances;
(d) Training and orientation or workers;
(e) Equal pay;
(f) Regulation of responsibility at work;
(g) Compensation for accidents, negligence and breach of duty of care in the work place.

As many areas of working environment are very broad, therefore there are many laws which are applicable. It is useful to refer to the Acts which regulate the work environment.

Factories Acts (1937, 1961), Health and Safety at Work Act (1974), Employment Protection Act (1978), Misuse of Drugs Act (1971), Mines and Quarries Act (1954), Occupiers Liability Act (1957), Employer's Liability Act (1969), Health and Safety at Work Act (Compulsory Insurance) (1974), Fire Safety of Places of Sports Act (1987), Consumers Protection Act (1987) and EPA (1990).

There are many Regulations in this concerns, in addition to the EEC Directives on Health and Safety at Work in accordance with Art. 118a of Maastricht Treaty which is the same provision of the Treaty of Rome (Art. 118a).

The new policy of the EEC which is based on Maastricht Treaty, especially the social policy enhances the care for workers and the improvement of work environment. It is clear that the EEC Directive on work environment demonstrates the improvement of social, economic and health environment of work.

Besides, taking the Directives in their totality there are many precautions which should be observed in order to protect the workers from the environmental risks and dangers at work and to ensure for them the best conditions of work environment.

---

[1] - The Times on 15.3.92 (Times Law Report)
[2] - The Times on 9.10.93. But the High Court in the case of Rudy Molinari v the Ministry of Defence (December 6, 1993) awarded the Plaintiff £163,000 compensation for suffering from leukaemia. Molinari was serving in a Nuclear Submarine and was exposed to radiation. The Times 7 December 1993.

Protection of the Environment

Among the important Directives are on: the Work Place,[1] The Use of Work Equipment,[2] the Use of Personal Protective Equipment,[3] the Manual Handling of Loads, the Display Screen Equipment (Visual Display Units). This Directive (90/270/EEC) provides for minimum safety and health requirements for work with Display Screen Equipment.[4]

The EEC Directive Related to Exposure to Carcinogens at Works (90/394) which are substances which cause cancer.[5]

And the EEC Directive on the Protection of Workers from risks Related to Exposure to Biological Agents at Work (90/679).[6]

Also the ILO activities in the fields of work environment are very important, there are many ILO conventions which protect the workers. One of the important legal instruments in this field is the Code of Practice on Safety and Health in Construction Industries.[7] This Code was approved by the Governing Body of the ILO at its 250th Session (May-June 1991).

---

[1] - This Directive on the minimum safety and Health Requirements for Workplace 89/654/EEC obligates the employer to keep all escape routes and emergency exits clean, the work place clean, to carry out maintenance and rectify faults as soon as possible and to check safety equipment and to observe the 2 annexes to the Directive. The Commission has amendement on this Directive, in a proposal in the light of the opinion of the European Parliament to extend the scope of the Directive on the means of transport Com (93)421 of 1 October 1993.

[2] - The Directive applies to all sectors of work activity and place on the employer responsibility for the health and safety of workers regarding the provision and use of all work equipment and to ensure that the equipment is suitable and properly adapted without risks to health and safety and adequately maintained. The work equipment must comply, for example:
. Control systems must be safe and breakdown/damage must not result in danger:
* Protection against rupture or disintegration of work equipment.
* Maintenance to be possible, when work equipment is shut down. If not possible, then measures to enable work to be carried out outside danger zones.
* This Directive provides, inter alia: the employer must assess the risk(s) posed: select PPE which gives protection against risk(s).

[3] - The equipment is suitable for the worker including fitting correctly, is compatible with the work:
. PPE must be free of charge, and be maintained in clean and good working order.
. Must provide information, instruction and training in the use of PPE.

[4] - It applies to all work stations with a display screen (with certain exceptions, e.g. driver's cab or control cab systems, onboard computer systems, portable use at work station, cash register).
Employers are required to analyse work stations to evaluate safety and health risks and take appropriate measures to eliminate the risks found, and to plan daily work on a display screen so that it is periodically interrupted by breaks or changes of activity.
Workers are entitled to an appropriate eye and sight test before starting display screen work, and assessment at regular intervals and if they experience visual difficulties attributable to the work they are entitled to an ophthalmological examination if the eye shows this necessary.

[5] - This Directive sets up a framework of protection for workers exposed to Carcinogens that requires:
An assessment of the risks of exposure, its nature and degree by the employer. Dependent on that assessment the Carcinogens must be replaced by a harmless or less dangerous substance or failing this be used in a closed system. Suitable procedures must be adopted in situations of abnormal exposure and emergency conditions. Monitoring and health surveillance procedures to be appropriate to the particular substance and type of exposure.

[6] - The Directive defines biological agents as micro-organisms in the broadest sense, including those which have been generally modifed, and cell cultures. It applies to all work activities in which workers may be exposed to biological agents, but makes important distinctions between activities where there is decision well considered to work with, eg microbiological laboratory work, and those where exposure may be incidental to work activity, health care, farming.

[7] - The Code of Practice is a document offering practical guidance on the policy and standard setting in occupational safety and health for use by governments, employers, workers and any other persons involved in construction.

Work Environment

This Code applies to many construction activities and fields.[1]

This Code of Practice states that the national competent authorities in modern States have to adopt national laws and legislations to ensure the safety and health of the workers employerd in construction industries and to protect them from all risks which would arise from the work environment.

The national laws and regulations should provide technical studies or codes of practice. These practices should have due regard to relevant standards adopted by recognised international organizations in the field of standardisation.

The Code of Practice deals with the safety of workplaces, fire prevention and fire fighting, lighting, scaffolds and ladders, design and construction, inspection and maintenance, lifting appliances on scaffolds, installation, examination and test, operation, hoists, derricks, tower cranes, lifting ropes, transport and health in construction, earth-moving, or materials-handling equipment, power shovels, excavators, steam shovels, bulldozers, mobile asphalt layers and finishers, plant, machinery, equipment and hand tools, pneumatic tools, engines, silos, concrete work equipment, pressure plant, conveyors, crusher plants, power generators, work at heights including roof work, work on tall chimneys, excavation, shafts, earthworks, underground works and tunnels, underground construction, fire protection, electricity, blasting, haulage, dust control, underground pipelines, cofferdams and caissons and work in compressed air, work in cofferdams and caissons, working chambers, man locks, air supply, signalling work in tunnels in compressed air, structural frames and concrete work, pile driving, work over water, boats, demolition (walls, floors, structural steelwork, tall chimneys), electricity (inspection, maintenance and testing), explosives (transport, storage and handling and disposal), health standards, first aid and occupational health services, hazardous substances, dangerous atmospheres, radiation hazards[2] ionising hazards, non ionising radiation, heat stress, cold and wet conditions, noise and vibration and biological agents.

The Code prohibits the destruction and disposal of waste on construction sites injurious to safety and health.

And also the Code provides for personal protective equipment and protective clothing where the employer should ensure the use of these protective equipment and clothing by workers in

---

[1] - The code applies to:-
(a) construction activities which cover:
(i) building, including excavation and the construction, structural alteration, renovation, repair, maintenance (including cleaning and painting) and demolition of all types of buildings or structures;
(ii) civil engineering, including excavation and the construction, structural alteration, repair, maintenance and demolition of, for example, airports, docks, harbours, inland waterways, dams, river and avalanche and sea defence works, roads, and highways, railways, bridges, tunnels, viaducts, and works related to the provision of services such as communicaitons, drainage, sewerage, water and energy supplies;
(iii) the erection and dismantling of prefabricated buildings and structures, as well as the manufacturing of prefabricated elements on the construction site;
(b) the fabrication and erection of oil rigs and offshore installations while under construction on shore.
Para. 1.2.2 - The provisions of this code should be considered as the basic requirements for protecting workers' safety and health.
Para. 1.2.3 - provides in the application of the code to self-employed persons as may be specified by national laws and regulations.
[2] - Section 17-6 on Radiation Hazards, the Code says: 'Stringent safety regulations should be drawn up and enforced by the competent authority with respect to construction industries for the protection of workers.' Safety and Health in Construction - International Labour Organisation - Geneva 1992.

Protection of the Environment

compliance with standards set by governments, and competent authorities and according to their regulations.

The workers should use proper protective equipment and clothing provided for them. They should be instructed to use them properly.

And finally, the Code sets up standards for welfare at every construction site as good drinking water, sanitary and washing facilities, cloakrooms, facilities for food and drinks, shelters and accommodation. Health and safety precautions should be always given important attention from all parties and the strict liability must be imposed.

The duty of care must be imperative in all circumstances which cause a threat to public safety and health, because the protection of public health and safety generally or concerning the work environment must be safeguarded and ensured in modern legislations.

iii   Food and the Protection of Consumers
1.   The Quality of Food and its Protection

Food or nourishment is everything that feeds the human body, the natural food, whether its source is animals or plants, the environment is the habitat of all living organisms.

Good environment produces good food, therefore the improvement of the quality of life necessitates the care for the environment, because it is the source of food, so it is necessary the improvement and the protection of the environment.

Food can be natural or artificial, that is, it can be produced from natural and synthetic elements. Human life and existence depend on food, therefore food technology became an important factor for both human life and environment, because both affect each other, that is, in order to produce good food, it is necessary to care for the environment, and for its part the environment affects the production of food and its safety.

So the preservation of habitats for both animals and plants is a straight way forward for the implementaiton of green policy for improving the human food and the quality of life.

And this is not an easy task, as there are thousands of biological species, eg. in England there are 30,000 animal species and 5,000 plant species.[1]

So in this study about food, it is necessary to concentrate on four points: food hygiene, the protection of food, food law and the availability of food.

a.   Food Hygiene

Food hygiene means care and observance of the standards of healthy food. Sometimes food chains make publicity about organic food 'as it is healthy food' which is safe from chemicals which damage the environment and the wildlife.[2]

So "organic" in this sense means using natural fertilisers (animals or plants) for the crop or using the method of crop rotation.[3]

Healthy food necessitates the care for the environment, cleaning it from pollutants which cause damage to the crop. Food chains insist on green care food, which is clean from bacteria, pests and chemicals which harm the health and safety.

b.   Protection of Food

Protection of food necessitates food watch and the control of its safety from dangerous risks, eg. bacteria, pests, pollution, radioactivity, chemicals, metals. Besides, there must be protection

---

[1] - DoE's pamphlet on (What can you do for the Environment?)
[2] - Sainsbury's pamphlet on the Environment. p. 10.
[3] - Ibid.

of food by good packaging.[1]

The protection of food needs always continuous and regular checks, control and scientific research into causes of food risks and dangers, whether chemicals, bacteria, radioactivity, metals or food poisoning. These need technical methods of checking defective food. Of course there must be studies, rules and regulations to ensure the food safety.

c. Food Law

The control of food safety necessitates making the necessary legislations to ensure the control and safeguard of the standards of food safety; hygiene and protection, without the law, the food safety would not be protected.[2]

The Food Safety Act (1990) in England and Wales[3] deals with food hygiene, protection and safety. In Part one of the Act, it defines food, as:-

Food includes:-

(a) drink

(b) articles and substances of no nutritional value which are used for human consumption;

(c) chewing gum and other products of a like nature and use; and

(d) articles and substances used as ingredients in the preparation of food or anything falling within this subsection.

While Para. (2) of this Section adds; food does not include:

(a) live animals or birds, or live fish which are not used for human consumption while they are alive;

(b) fooder or feeding stuffs for animals, birds or fish;

(c) controlled drugs within the meaning of the Mis-use of Drugs Act 1971; or

(i) medicinal products within the meaning of the Medicine Act 1968 in respect of which product licences within the meaning of that Act are for the time being in force; or

(ii) other articles or substances in respect of which licences are for the time being in force in pursuance of orders under Section 104 or 105 of that Act (application of the Act to other articles and substances).

Besides, the Act empowers the Ministers (Agriculture, Fisheries and Food, the Secretary of State for Health) to function for implementing this Act.

In the Schedule attached to the Act, under S. 16(1), there are provisions for prohibiting or regulating the sale, possession for sale, or offer, exposure or advertisement for sale, of any specified substance or of any substance of any specified class, with a view to its use in the preparation of food.

And in Para. 2(1) of this Section, the Act deals with fitness of food.

The Act regulates the use in the manufacture of product for sale for such consumption, of food derived from a food source which is suffering or has suffered from, or which is liable to be suffering or to have suffered from, any disease specified in the regulations.

Section 2(2) provides:

provision for prohibiting or regulating, or the enabling enforcement authorities to prohibit or regulate

---

[1] - Ministry of Agriculture. Food Safety Department. Food Protection. 4 Food Sense. 1992.

[2] - Food requirements according to Food Safety Act are: (a) not injurious to health, (b) fit for human consumption, (c) not contaminated.

[3] - Halisbury Statutes No. 18. Butterworths 1991.

Protection of the Environment

(a) the sale for human consumption; or
(b) the offer, exposure of distribution for sale for such consumption, of shellfish taken from beds or other layings for the time being designed by or under the regulations.

S. 3(1) Provides for regulating generally the treatment and disposal of food -
(a) which is unfit for human consumption, or
(b) which, though not unfit for human consumption, is not intended for, or is prohibited from being sold for, such consumption.

d. The Availability of Food

The availability of food depends on agriculture, animals husbandry and the production of food. It is difficult to say that food is available and abundant to all peoples of the world. If food is available to the developed, industrial and rich countries, but to great number of the developing and poor countries, food is not available, and many people face hunger and poverty.

To make food available to all peoples, is not easy, and to make them satisfy their need for food, is like thinking of Utopia.

The availability of food depends on the environment, the improvement of agriculture, animals husbandry, improvement of the production of food industries, using modern methods of technology and also the end of wars, conflicts, local hostilities and the creation of mass consciousness for the need to produce food for the needy and their consumption, especially the Third World and the improvement of the economies of the underdeveloped countries, especially in Africa where there are still civil wars and local hostilities.

The Advisory Panel on Food Security (APFS) said in its Report on the African Food crisis that it is necessary to promote substantial food security in many developing countries which have environmental degradation and hazards, severe debt burdens and social unrest. These countries need technical know-how and food security.[1]

The Report calls upon the UN to add **substantial livelihood of all** in its Declaration on Human Rights.[2]

Of course, the international community should take the necessary legal measures and put the foundation which secures food and technical assistance for the production of food for the livelihood of the poor and hungry peoples in the Third World. International law of the environment should bind all members of the international community to cooperate and promote the availability of food, technical means and science for the development of the production of food in the poor countries in order to secure their livelihood, the basic essentials of food and the subsistance of the hungry peoples.

The **World Commission on Environment and Development** in its Report said 'global food security depends also on ensuring that all peoples, even the poorest of the poor, can get. While on world scale this challenge requires a reappraisal of global food distribution, the task weighs more imemdiately and heavily on national governments. Inequitable distribution of production assets, unemployment and under-employment are the heart of the problem of hunger in many

---

[1] - **Food 2000 - Report of the World Commission on Environment and Development.** Zed Books 1987. p. 97.

[2] - Ibid. p. 100.

EEC Directive on Product Liability

countries.[1]

The WCED has suggested in its strategy for substantial food security some solutions for ensuring global food security, e.g. governments intervention in agriculure to increase investment in agricultural sector and research, the support of farmers, increasing the export of food for the needy countries, lifting the trade barriers and increasing food supply to poor countries, at fair prices, land use for agriculture, water management and the use of more organic plant nutrients instead of chemicals which ensure less dependance on chemicals as fertilizers.[2]

2. Protection of the Consumers

The protection of the consumers is very necessary, regarding the protection of their lives, health and safety from produced goods other than their food which is regulated by Food Safety Act (1990), its principles have been explained in the previous pages.

i. EEC Directive on Product Liability

The main features of the protection of consumers are embodied in the Product Liability (under Part 1) of the Consumer Protection Act (1987). The product liability under this Act is in compliance with the EEC Directive on Product Liability (of 25 July 1985) which is, according to Art. 22, addressed to the Member-States. Art. 19 binds the Member-States to take the necessary measures to legislate (laws, regulations and provisions) in order to comply with this Directive.

The EEC Directive has been embodied in the Product Liability (Part 1) of the Consumer Protection Act.

ii. Product Liability Act

The Act defines 'Product' as any goods or electricity and (subject to sub-section (3) below) includes a product which is comprised in another product, whether by virtue of being a component part or raw material or otherwise.

While the same Act defines 'Producer' in relation to product:-

(a)   the person who manufactured it;

(b)   in case of a substance which has not been manufactured, won or an abstracted but essential characteristics of which are attributable to an industrial or other process having been carried out (for example, in relation to agricultural produce), the person who carried out that process.

The Act regards, in S.2(1), the person liable for damage from a defect in product is:-

(a)   the producer of the product;

(b)   any person who, by putting his name on the product or using a trade mark or other distinguishing mark in relation to the product, has held himself out to be the producer of the product;

(c)   any person who has imported the product into a Member State from a place outside the Member-States in order, in the course of any business of his, to supply it to another.

The Act regards a 'defet' in the product if 'its 'safety' is not such as, persons generally are entitled to expect, and for those purposes' safety' in relation to a product, shall include safety with respect to product comprised in that product and safety in the context of risks of damage to property, as well as in the context of risks of death or personal injury (S.3/1).

---

[1] - **The World Commission on Environment and Development. Our Common Future.** Oxford University Press. 3rd Ed. 1988. p. 129.

[2] - Ibid. pp. 130-135.

Protection of the Environment

S.5/1 of the Act defines 'damage' as death or personal injury or any loss of or damage to any property (including land).
Part II of the Act deals with 'Consumer Safety':-
S.10-(1) A person shall be guilty of an offence if he-
(a) supplies any consumer goods which fail to comply with the general safety requirements;
(b) offers or agree to supply any such goods; or
(c) exposes or processes any such goods for supply.
(2) For the purposes of this Section consumer goods fail to comply with the general safety requirements, if they are not reasonably safe having regard to all circumstances, including;
    (a) in the manner in which, and purposes of which, the goods are being or would be marketed, the get-out of the goods, the use of any mark in relation to the goods and any instructions or warnings which are given or would be given with respect to the keeping, use or consumption of the goods;
    (b) any standards of safety published by any person either for goods of a description which applies to the goods in question or for matters relating to goods of that description, and
    (c) the existence of any means by which it would have been reasonable (taking into account the cost, likelihood and extent of any inprovement) for the goods to have been made safer.
S.11 of the Act grants the Secretary of State the powers to make 'Safety Regulations' concerning consumer's goods. This Section gives details of the nature of these regulations in order to protect the safety of goods and the consumers and the implementation of these regulations.[1]

d - Noise and Nuisance

Noise is vibration which causes vexation and nuisance, and so, is regarded as one of the dangerous causes of damage which need control.
Noise is dangerous to health and public safety as it affects the hearing, the work,[2] sleep and rest. People are always worrried of noise especially, from noise of transport and aircraft.[3]
Nuisance is a broad term which includes noise and other environmental problems as those mentioned in S. 79 of EPA (1990) which are Smoke (Para.(1)b), Fumes or Gases (Para.(1)c),

---

[1] - The EEC Commission has published a 'Green Paper' on "**...Guarantees for Consumers Goods and After Sales Services.**" The purpose of this paper is to harmonize Community Law, regarding after sales obligations of the producer, especially goods which affect the public health and safety. p. 25. Com (93) 509 of 15.11.93

[2] - The UN Convention Concerning the Protection of Workers against Occupational Hazard in the Working Environment Due to Air Pollution, Noise and Vibration, Art. 3(1) defines 'Noise' covers all sound which can result in hearing impairment or be harmful or otherwise dangerous.
Art. 11(1) imposes a duty on the Member-States and their competent authorities to supervise the circumstances and conditions in which the workers are exposed to noise, vibration in the working environment. Supervision should include a pre-assignment medical examination and periodical examinations. Para. 3 of the same Article provides that the Member-States have to provide a suitable employment for th worker as alternative to which that exposes them to the danger of noise, or 'maintain their Social Security benefits.
Art.12 of the same Convention provides that any use of processes, substances and machinery equipment which involve exposure of workers to noise or vibration must be notified to the competent authority of the Member-State as appropriate which may prescribe the conditions of use or the prohibition. Kiss. Selected Multilateral Treaties in the Field of the Environment. UN Environmental Programme. Series 3. 1983. pp. 482-3.

[3] - The Control of Nuisance in France was first regulated by Royal Decree on 15 October 1810, mentioning the establishments which cause pollution and nuisance. Kiss. La Prótection Internationale de L'Environnement. Documentaire Francaise. 17 Octobre 1977. p. 7.

Noise

Dust, Steam, Smell or other effluvia (Para.(1)d).

Also this Section has included any accumulation or deposit, animal or noise emitted from premises prejudicial to health, as Statutory Nuisance under the EPA.

Both nuisance and noise, generally and particularly, are dangerous to health and environment and regarded as a kind of pollution. Therefore modern legislation tends to protect the individual and the public from nuisance and noise.

Regarding the EEC law, the Council adopted the Directive of 1986 on 'the Protection of Workers from Noise'[1]

The European Community measures aimed at the protection of the citizens from noise and setting maximum noise emmissions from products, e.g. motor vehicles, motor cycles, aircraft, tractors, plant and equipment, lawnmowers and household appliances.[2]

The High Court ruling on 29.9.93 in the Action of Anti-Noise Campaign v DoT (Department of Transport) said that DoT plans to change the night flight increased the number of airplanes to land at Heathrow Airport at night and so unlawful and not allowed by Civil Aviation Act (1982) in order to control the level of noise at night. This judgment supports the anti-noise campaign against night flights.[3]

Also in another case, Regina v Secretary of State for Transport, Exparte Richmond upon Thames, London Borough Council and others in the Queen's Bench Division, the Court said that the new rules for controlling night flying which the Secretary of State for Transport planned to introduce at Heathrow, Gatwick and Stansted airports were unlawful. They sought to determine the number of permissible flights by reference to a noise based quota count assigned to each aircraft type, rather than by imposing a ceiling on the number of aircraft movements as required by Section 78(3b) of the Civil Aviation Act (1982).[4]

The protection of the public from noise is very necessary as an unacceptable level of noise violates the law and the EPA protects the people from noise which is a kind of environmental pollution.[5]

Moreover, the DoE has published a guide on Green Rights and Responsibilities. It said the DoT is responsible for controlling aircraft and helicopter flight noise at Heathrow, Gatwick and Stansted airports and the citizens can complain about flight noise and if they suffered from noise can claim compensation. The Local Authorities (Councils) take the necessary measures to deal with the complaints.

If the citizens cannot get satisfaction they can bring a civil action in court for damage, loss or injury.[6]

Regarding the worry of the public from the flight noise the Informer said that the authorities, whether at Heathrow Airport or at the DoT, always monitored flight noise and made investigations into complaints with good attention. Also Heathrow Airport Authority called upon

---

[1] - EEC Directive requires companies to provide details of noise levels, these conform with norms established by international standards bodies. European Documentation on Environmental Policy of EEC. Ibid.

[2] - Ibid.

[3] - The Informer on 1.10.93.

[4] - The Times Law Report (12.10.93).

[5] - Miss London (22.11.93), the magazine, said that Hackney Local Council received 4,000 complaints of noise last year (1992).

[6] - DoT. Green Rights and Responsibilities.

Protection of the Environment

airlines for investment in technology to minimise noise.[7]

Moreover, the claimant of noise damage can request from the local authorities for control of noise and to take the preventative measures to stop its sources. He can also bring his/her case before the court under the EPA and request for compensation.[2]

e - Pollution

International law of the environment puts great responsibility on the State to protect the environment from pollution and calls upon all States to cooperate in this task for the protection of the environment locally, regionally and globally.

Pollution worries evreyone, whether environmentalists or others, as it always threatens the environment, the living resources (animals and plants) the ecology and the atmosphere.

Many books and studies have been written about pollution, and the damage it causes to the environment. So there is no need to repeat what has been said or written, but the study should concentrate on the best effective action the States and the international community should do to protect the environment from pollution.

i - What is Pollution?

In a few words, there must be a useful definition of pollution.

Pollution is the contamination of the environment by any elements or factors which damage its purity.

It is not necessary that pollution is caused by man or any human action, deliberately or not. Pollution can take place by any natural elements or factors. The environment can be polluted by decaying animals, plants, waste or various poisonous substances which can affect the purity of the environment. It is natural phenomena.[3]

The concern is about harmful pollution which creates damage to the environment. This pollution can contaminate the atmosphere, the air, the sea, rivers and land. It can also happen to affect not only a small region within the jurisdiction of the State, but its damage extends to territories of other States or can affect the global environment, as the pollution caused by the Chernobyl disaster, or any radiation which can go beyond a State's territory which is goverened by the Convention on Long Range Transboundary Air Pollution of 13 November 1979, signed in Geneva. Such pollution happens to be at such a distance which can be a long range air pollution which needs multinational efforts to combat and to cooperate in order to protect the environment.[4]

Also the danger which atmospheric pollution creates, such as acid rain which affects the ecosystems when the air is polluted by acids which are carried by wind for thousands of miles and which affects many countries.[5]

There is no doubt that natural pollution may be more dangerous to the environment than man-made pollution but, from the legal point of view, man-made pollution is one which international law of the environment can regulate. It can put the rules which prevent or call upon the

---

[1] - The Informer on 29.9.93 and The Leader on 24.2.94.

[2] - **Simon Ball and Stuart Bell.** Ibid. p. 255.

[3] - **T.J. McLoughlin** defines pollution as: 'the introduction of man of waste matter or surplus energy into the environment which directly or indirectly causes damage to man and his environment other than himself as quoted by H.M. Dix. Environmental Pollution. John Wiley & Sons. 1981.

[4] - See Arts. (1-4) of the Convention. Also the UN Anti Pollution Treaty of 16 September 1987 signed in Montreal by the EEC, US and many other developed countries. Also the International Convention on the Prevention of Pollution from Ships, of 1973, the Convention on Intervention on the High Seas, in Cases of Oil Polution Casualties (1969).

[5] - **Mark Carwardine. The WWF Environment..** Optima. 1990. pp. 22-23.

Pollution

international community to control or to be on alert to stop its occurance or to take precautions regarding the measures which should be taken in order to notify the neighbouring or other countries of the danger which may come of it.

In fact, the danger of pollution, whether it happens on land, air, sea or may be atmospheric, biological, chemical or nuclear, needs regional, international and global cooperation in order to prevent, control or minimise its effects on the atmosphere otherwise its atmospheric or biological effect would be great to cause damage to the global environment.

The most global pollution is caused by the increase in CO_2 which is released by fossil fuel, e.g. oil, coal and natural gas.[1]

Moreover, according to EC statistics, pollution costs billions of ECU yearly, the estimated damage in France is ECU 1.4bn in 1982 for water purification and the damage to buildings amounted to ECU 2.7bn per year.

Besides, the damage to industrial and economic activities and forests was estimated at ECU 300m in 1986.[2]

So the State's duty is to protect the environment from pollution cannot be minimized, as the pollution of national environment has great effect on the international and global environment. The role of the State in the protection of the environment against pollution appears in so many legislations at the national level in the UK Acts in the field of pollution. So it is necessary to look at them.

ii. UK Acts on Pollution

There are different Acts which deal with pollution, e.g. **Control of Pollution Act** (1974), **EPA** (1990),[3] **Road Traffic Act** (1988),[4] **Radioactive Materials Act** (1991),[5] and **The Clean Air Act** (1993).[6]

Taking into consideration the role of the State in the protection of the environment against all kinds of pollution, it has an effective role in combating pollution, because the State has a law-making function, by making laws which protect the environment, it implements them and monitors the actions of the individuals, legal persons, firms and corporations which pollute the environment. The State is the important subject of the enviromental law whether at national or

---

[1] - Kenneth Mellanby. **The Biology of Pollution.** 2nd Ed. Edward Arnold. 1980. pp. 4-5.

[2] - Environment Policy in the European Community. Office for the Offical Publications of the European Communities. 92. p. 13.

[3] - S.70 of the Act deals with Air Pollution and S.79 deals with causes of the Air Pollution and the protection of Clean Air from pollution and nuisance.

[4] - The Road Traffic Act deals with the control of pollution from Vehicle emissions of pollutants.

[5] - The Radioactive Materials Act (Road Transport) S.2 deals with the control of transporting radioactive materials which cause danger to public safety.

[6] - S.3 of **The Clean Air Act** defines dark smoke which causes pollution of the air, as "dark or darker than shade 2 on the chart". So the Act prohibits the dark smoke and it is an offence to cause the emission of dark smoke. Ss. 30-33 deal with the information about the air pollution from dark smoke and S.34 deals with the duty of local authorities (Councils) to investigate and research on "the air pollution and their responsibilities concerning monitoring the emission of dark smoke".
See also the Hounslow Environmental Charter of February 1993 which deals with the responsibility of Hounslow Borough Council under the EPA (1990). Under (to minimise pollution) the Charter says: "We have:
* established pollution monitoring system, control of noise pollution and established noise monitoring system to minimise noise from aircraft, continue to oppose any increase in night flights out of Heathrow
* to minimise water pollution.
* monitoring water quality and drinking water, etc. ...."

Protection of the Environment

international level [1]

f - Water

Water, air, food and heat are the essentials for life. Without them life cannot be sustained. So water affects the ecology and environment enormously, to this effect, civilized society began, since a long time, to give great consideration to the purity of water and its hygiene.

Water demonstrates the need for good management and global strategy.[2]

As water is very important in any environmental study whether at national or international level, but in this topic, the sutdy will concentrate on the internal measures the State takes in order to protect the purity of water, while the sea pollution will be discussed in Chapter 3, which relates more to international law of the environment.

Therefore, the water in internal law (inland waters) takes its importance from the need of the population and the care for the purity of rivers, streams, underground streams, canals, lakes, reservoirs, water industry (drinking water), pools and the water for bath and swimming.

i. Water Acts in the U.K.

There are several Water Acts, since 1971, S.2 of the Prevention of Oil Pollution Act (1971) provides: ' It is an offence if a person discharges of oil into UK waters'. Also the discharge of oil from pipelines as a result of exploration is an offence.

S.11 provides that it is a duty to report discharge of oil into waters of harbours. The Water Act of 1973 has well organized the water management in order to control water treatment, supply, sewage, land drainage, flood, pollution, inland fisheries and water for recreational uses and ecological matters, besides the establishment of water authorities.[3]

The Reservoirs Act of 1975 defines 'reservoirs' if it is designed to hold, or capable of holding water above the natural level of any part of the land adjoining the reservoir and layer raised reservoir to hold or capable of holding more than 25,000 cubic meters of water above that level. Also the Water Acts of 1981, 1987, 1989 and the Water Industry Act of 1991. S.54 of the Water Act (1981) provided that the duty of undertaker of water supply:

a. to provide supply of water to any premises.

b. to maintain a connection between a water main and a service pipe by which such a supply is provided.[4]

ii. Rivers

The EPA (1990) has authorized the NRA controlling of rivers pollution, maintaining and improving water quality in rivers and coastal waters. It monitors water quality by taking and

---

[1] - See Pollution topic in Chapter 3, Section (1).

[2] - 25,000 people die every day because of water mis-management and two-thirds of the world population suffer from not having sanitary water for drinking. Kiss. **Droit International de l'Environnemen. Documentation Française.t** 1992. p 26.

[3] - See the EEC Directive 76/464 on the protection of water from the dangerous substances as toxic, organohalogens, onganophosphorous, mercury or lead. Member States take measures to eliminate the pollution of water and establish the system of monitoring the emission of substances and limited values. Kiss. Ibid.

[4] - This Act also provides that:-

S. 68 The duties of the udnertaker:

- to ensure the quality of the water is wholesome.

S. 69 to preserve water quality regulation and monitor water supply.

S. 70 provides that it is an offence to supply water unfit for human consumption and S. 71 provides that it is an offence by causing pollution to water resources from waste, or if a person causes water to run to waste from well, borehole or other work. Also S. 72 protects water supply from contamination.

Drinking Water

analysing samples from points all over the country throughout the year.[1]
The most important thing is the control of the purity of water which the different water Acts have intended since the introduction of water distribution system.
The control of water pollution was and is the important issue concerning the purity of water and supply of clean water under Rivers (Prevention of Pollution Act 1951) and the Act of 1961 which brought more control of water discharge in rivers and estuaries, besides, the Water Reservoirs Act of 1963 which extended the control on underground water.[2]
The NRA was created by the Water Act (1989) to ensure more control on quality of water and to apply the system of public control (discharge consents).[3] Of course the control of pollution and monitoring the quality of water are the main purposes of the NRA.[4]

iii. **EEC Water Directives**

The EEC adopted several Directives on Water. The purposes of these Directives are to ensure the quality of drinking water (Surface Water Directive) the protection of inland and coastal waters against pollution and the protection of the consumers by ensuring that national authorities of the Member-States ensure clean water for the population and consumers.[5]

a - **Drinking Water**

The ECJ in Case No. C-337/89 (European Commission v UK in its judgment of 25 November 1992 said: 'The Directive on the quality of drinking water required Member-States to ensure that certain results were achieved and except with the limits of derogation laid down, they might not rely on special circumstances in order to justify a failure to discharge that obligation.[6]
Moreover the Court added that by failing to implement and to apply the Directive correctly, the UK had failed to fulfil its obligations under the EEC Treaty.[7]
It seems from the Court judgment that the Directive on the quality of drinking water is mandatory and the Member-States have to implement in their national legal order to protect the consumer, which is an obligation under the EEC Treaty.
In another case (Regina v Secretary of State for the Environment Ex Parte Friends of the Earth Ltd and Another[8], Queen's Bench Division). The Court said in its judgment of 29.3.94: 'Although the UK was in breach of its obligation to ensure water intended for human consumption met EEC standards of wholesomeness, it was sufficient for the Secretary of State for the environment to fulfil his duty to remedy that breach by accepting undertaking from water authorities to ensure confromity with those standards.'

---

[1] - DoE. Green Rights and Responsibilities. Ibid. pp. 22-23.
[2] - **Ball and Bell.** Ibid. p. 299.
[3] - DoE. Ibid.
[4] - National Rivers Authority v Alfred McAlpine Homes East Ltd. Case (Queen's Bench Divisional Court) in which the Court said in its judgment of 20.1.94 "In attaching liability to a building company for pollution.....it was sufficient that those immediately responsible on the site ...." It seems that the Court put the responsibility on the employer for rivers pollution caused by his employee.
[5] - In a case reported by the Informer on 1.4.94 in which the Hounslow Trading Standards Authority seized a number of 'Everest' mineral water bottles which contained tap water which did not have the hygiene standards of drinking water. The accused was fined £5,000 by the Feltham Magistraite Court.
[6] - TLR 10.12.92.
[7] - Art. 18(1) of the Council Directive 80/778/EEC of 15 July 1981 relating to the Quality of Water for human consumption (Official Journal 1980 1229. p. 11, required the Member-States to bring into force the laws, regulations and administrative provisions to comply with the Directive and its annexes .... and Art. 14 of the Directive provided that Member-States shall take the necessary measures to ensure that the quality of water intended for human consumption ...."
[8] - TRL 4.4.94.

But the Court did not envisage the obligation of the UK regarding the water supply under the (Regulation Water Quality (S) 1989 No. 1147) is so tight that the Secretary of State for the Environment would not be given time to 'take all such steps as appeared to him ... for the time being to be appropriate.' In the Court's opinion the words 'for the time being' envisaged a continuing monitoring duty.

The Court has accepted the monitoring duty for the part the Member-States regarding the water quality, when the water supplied by separate undertakings (water utilities or services - third parties) to fulfil the obligation of the Member-States under Water Supply Regulations, is enough to ensure conformity which the standards of water quality, as when the Secretary of State sees insufficient progress, so he can make use of his powers and he had to make an enforcement order.[1]

b - Bathing Water Directive

The EEC Directive on the Quality of Bathing Water OJ/976/31 which ensures that the quality of bathing water (beaches and coastal waters) conforms to the standards put by the Directive No. 76/160/EEC of 8 December 19976. Arts. 2 and 3 of the Directive require that Member-States should set the limit values applicable to bathing water for the physical, chemical and microbiological parameters indicated in the annex of the Directive.

ECJ in the case C56/90 The European Commission v UK, said in its judgment of 14 December 1993: "The Directive on the quality of bathing water required Member-States to take steps to ensure that certain results were attained and, apart from the derogations expressly permitted by the Directive, they could not rely on particular circumstances to justify a failure to fulfil that obligation".[2]

So the Court declared that by failing to take all necessary measures to ensure that the quality of bathing waters in Blackpool and of those adjacent to Southport conformed to the limit values set in accordance with Article 3 of the Council Directive 76/160/EEC of 8 December 1975 concerning the quality of bathing water, the United Kingdom had failed to fulfil its obligations under the EEC Treaty.[3]

B - The Individual

The role of the individual is not less than that of the State's. Although the State is the dominant factor in the protection of the environment, as it is powerful, it can make laws and implement them and call upon the individuals to respect and do not violate them, the individuals can act positively or negatively, regarding the environment.

The individual can act against the protection of the environment, he/she can damage, pollute or contaminate it.

Modern international law of the environment is addressed to the individuals as well as States. And by their cooperation the environment can be protected and generally speaking the global environment would be safe.

---

[1] - Queen's Bench Division Judgment. Ibid.
[2] - TLR. 15 July 1993.
[3] - Ibid.

The Role of the Individual

Two successive Environment Secretaries in Britain agreed that individuals have an important role in the protection of the environment.[1]

The individual has rights and responsibilities under the law of the environment, so he/she is a subject and object of the law. This means that the environmental legal rules are addressed to the individual, they confer rights upon the individuals and bind them at the same time. The individual has interest in the protection of the environment, as he/she benefits from the environment, if the quality of life in a good environment improves, the individuals will enjoy good living. On the other hand, the individual can do damage to the environment, either by his/her negligence, omission, negatively by not acting in the proper way to protect the environment, or positively by causing intentionally or unintentionally damage to the environment, and so inflicting harm to other human beings or the fauna and flora and the habitat. So modern international law of the environment regards the individual as an active subject next to the State, in participating in the development of law and the protection and improvement of the environment.

The role of the individuals cannot be ignored. It is an important and active factor, whether positive or negative in the protection and in drawing the policy of the green environment all over the world. This appears in the green movements all over the world, where the green parties which are groups of individuals, nowadays have an effective role in caring for the environment and putting pressure on governments to sustain fair policies for the protection of the environment and combating all kinds of pollution.

As the individual is an important subject of the law of the environment, so those who concern with it, whether natural, legal persons, international governmental, non-governmental organisations or States and the international community call upon the individual to care for the environment and to play his/her part in the protection of the environment, because the individual role is very effective. In the developed countries, where the citizens have good educational standards, the environment is more protected by the participation of the individuals than the countries of the Third World and the underdeveloped countries.

The DoE in Britain recognising the role of the individual has clearly manifested this role in proclaiming the green rights and responsibilities of the individuals by enhancing their role and calling upon the citizens to participate effectively in the protection of the environment and the implementation of the green policy,[2] as the citizen benefits from the protection and the improvement of the environment and accordingly, he/she has environmental rights and at the same time he/she is responsible for the protection of the environment in case of causing damage to it.

Regarding the role of the individual, it is not only recognised under national law but also under international law e.g.; the European Convention (CoE) on the Civil Liability for Damage

---

[1] - Michael Heseltine: 'Government provides the law and institutions within which we can exercise our environmental rights and discharge our responsibilities. But unless each one of us plays our own part no amount of lawmaking will make any difference to the quality of the environment'. DoE. Green Rights and Responsibilities. Ibid. P.3. Michael Howard: 'I do not believe that it would be right for the Government alone to determine the content of our CO_2 programme. Business and individuals can make a significant contribution by their own actions'. DoE. Climate Change. A Discussion Document. 1992. P.1.

[2] - National Westminster Bank. Environment Review 1993. It said the individuals count for their valuable contributions for the preservation and conservation of the environment and its protection against pollution. P.5. DoE. Green Rights and Responsibilities. Ibid.

Resulting from Activities Dangerous to Environment; this Convention has clearly provided that the individual has rights and obligations under the Convention.[1]

C - Industrial Enterprises, Corporations and Firms

Industrial and economic activities have great effect on the environment, especially when these activities create waste and materials which pollute the environment.

Cities and places which involve industry and economic development enterprises are always vulnerable to pollution of the environment. Big industrial factories, chemical works, atomic energy enterprises and even food industries create dangerous waste which causes pollution and damage to the environment.

So industrial enterprises, corporation and firms like the individuals produce dangerous materials, operate or exercise activities; inter alia, affect the environment in one way or the other. These activities may cause damage or produce waste dangerous to the environment, and so they are like the individuals would be liable for any dangerous activity which causes damage to the environment.

On the other hand, many industrial enterprises, corporations and firms may contribute to the protection of the environment and play a big role in exploiting science and technology for the protection of the environment.

So any industrial enterprises, corporations, or firms, would bear liability when causing damage to the environment, whether this damage is caused by negligence, fault in control or as a result of creating dangerous waste which pollutes the environment. Therefore these industrial enterprises, corporations and firms are liable for polluting the environment and bear full responsibility under the legal maxim: environmental pollution liability, "Polluter Pays".

Section 2 - The Role of International Community

The role of international community in the protection of the environment is well expressed in the few words of Maurice Strong the Secretary General of the UNCED in the foreword of the Global Partnership.[2] As he said: "The global partnership is essential to set the world community on to a new course for more sustainable, secure and equitable future as we move to the 21st Century."

These words express the importance of the role of international community as a whole for the protection of the environment, because the global environment concerns all peoples of the world. All have duty to protect the environment, because all would benefit from the partnership of working together for the protection and improvement of the environment.

Good and healthy environment will give milk and honey for all peoples of the world where there will be sustainable development and full integration of the environmental resources and the peoples of the world will share the benefits of these resources from their partnership and the environmental protection which will ensure secure and equitable share for all humankind.

---

[1] - See Art. 7. of the Convention and Art. 18.
[2] - United Nations. A guide to 21 Agenda 'Global Partnership'. UNCED. Geneva 1992.

The Role of International Community

Principles 9 and 22 of the Rio Declaration on the Environment and Development echo the importance of the role of the international community in the protection of the environment.[1] The Global environment imposes a duty on all humankind to protect and develop and so from the cooperation of the international community as a whole, all will benefit from this cooperation. The Rio Declaration has well expressed the environmental goal: 'With the goal of establishing a new and equitable global partnership through the creation of new levels of cooperation among States, key sectors of societies and peoples...'.

It is the international community as a whole which bears the great responsibility for the protection of the global environment. Because the entire States and peoples of the world can ensure by their cooperation the fulfilment of the strategy for care and protection of the environment, this community has collectively the means and resources which help any States and people to fulfil the global environment strategy.

The international community role in the environmental strategy was well embodied in the principle 27 of the Rio Declaration, it provided: 'States and people shall cooperate in good faith and in a spirit of partnership in the fulfilment of the principles embodied in this Declaration and in the further development of international law in the field of sustainable development.' And therefore it is necessary to deal in this Section with:-

A. The UN and other International Organisations.
B. The Universal Action.

A. The UN and International Organisations
1. UN System

Since its creation the UN created a global consciousness of the environment. The environment became one of the important issues which the UN and its system cared and is caring for.

The UN activities regarding the environment have important aspects: the first is that it brought the attention of the world community to the importance of environmental issues and so the environment became the focus of the international community. And second, it coordinated the efforts of the States, its Members, to the treaty making law on the environment, and third it created specialised Organisations for the environment e.g. UNEP and UNCED, and fourth, the introduction of sound scientific and technological system for use in the environmental problems. The UN efforts have achieved great progress in holding several international conferences on the environment. The Stockholm Conference on the Environment (5-16 June 1972) was a magnificant achievement which ended with a Declaration on Principles of the International Law of the Environment and became the cornerstone of the development of modern international law of the environment.

Also the GA has adopted several legal instruments on the environment, e.g. the World Charter for Nature (Res. 37/7 (1983) and Res. 45.53 (89)) on the Protection of Global Climate for Present and Future Generations of Mankind, in which the GA recognised the climate change as the common concern of mankind and urged States and the international Community to treat the climate change as priority issue and to collaborate in making every effort to prevent detrimental

---

[1] - Principle 22 provides: 'Indigenous people and their communities have a vital role in environmental management and development because of their knowledge and traditional practices. States should recognise and duly support their identity, culture and enable their effective participation in the achievement of sustainable development.'

Protection of the Environment

effects on climate and any activities which affect the ecological balance.[2]

It must be mentioned that the UN and its specialised Agencies have elaborated and concluded under their auspices more than 140 international conventions and treaties on the environment since the Declaration of Stockholm Conference (1972) over double the number of conventions concluded in 50 year period previously.[2]

This magnificent development of the treaty law on environment manifests a great achievement of the UN system on the international environment law.

Also this great progress has specifically been achieved by great efforts and contribution and collaboration of UNEP, UNCED and other UN Family Organisation, the IMO, UNESCO and FAO which coordinated their efforts with the UN in developing international environmental law.[3]

The contribution of the UN system to environmental law has been focused on Strategy (planning), Management, Conferences[4], and the codification of conventions, agreements and treaties on environmental matters.

It is great achievement of the UN system in developing modern international law of the environment and the formulation of its principles which form a great heritage of humankind for our generation and the future generations.

By the contribution of the UN system, the environment became a daily issue of the international community as a whole.

Also it is necessary to mention the role of the UNEP, as it carried the great burden of the work which has been accomplished by the UN system and its contribution to the development of environmental science, law, study, international cooperation, planning and drawing international environmental strategy.

UNEP dedicated much effort for the protection of the ozone layer by signing the Convention on the Protection of Ozone Layer in Vienna in March 1985. Afterwards UNEP succeeded in signing another important Protocol on the Substances that Deplete the Ozone layer (Montreal 1987) which has great international support by the joining of 62 States and the EEC to the Protocol.

In many areas of the environment the UNEP did good achievement with the cooperation of UNESCO, IPCC, WMO, WCIP, FAO, UNCOD, OECD, EEC, ECA, OAU, UNCED which led to the elaboration of different international conventions on environmental matters which concern the States and peoples of the world. The Areas which have been subject to these

---

[1] - Martin Dixon and Robert McCooquodale. Cases and Materials on International Law. Blackstone Press. 1991. PP.466-7.

[2] - UNEP. UNEP Profile. Nairobi. 1990.

[3] - The Treaties and Conventions since 1933 can be classified into the following categories: Preservation, Wildlife, Whale and Seal Catching, Fisheries, Protection of Birds, Pollution, Conservation of Living Resources and Plants, Cooperation, Protection of Workers, Liability in the field of Nuclear Energy and Damage, Protection of Rivers, Seas and Oceans against Pollution, Banning Nuclear Weapons Tests in the Atmosphere, Navigation, Combating Locust, Restriction on the Use of Detergents in Washing and Cleaning Products, Protection of Animals, Protection of Heritage, Archaelogical, Cultural and Artistic Materials, Dumping, Prohbition of Development, Production and Stockpiling of Biological, Bacteriological and Toxin Weapons and Their Destruction, Hazardous Wastes, Protection of the Environment, Energy, Continental Shelf, High Seas, Settlement of Disputes, Exploration of the Seas, Outer Space and Celestial Bodies, Civil Liability for Damage of Pollution, Nuclear Energy Tests and Accidents, Protection of Ozone Layer, and the Ban of Chemical Weapons Convention (1993).

[4] - John McCormack. The Global Environmental Movement. Belhaven Press.

conventions are: climate change, the Ozone layer, waste, marine environment, water, land degradation, forests, biological diversity, industry, energy, human settlement, health, the earth and its elemental cycles, earthwatch, chemicals, education and training, law, development, planning, cooperation and technical and financial assistance and public awareness and funding.[1] For its part, the GATT played its role in stressing the necessity of achieving environmental protection in the field of international trade and commerce and the prohibition of importing or exporting products which harm and do damage to the environment.

While FAO has adopted a code of conduct on the Use of Pesticide and the London Guidelines for the Exchange of Information on Chemicals in International Trade.[2]

The UN Conference at Rio de Janeiro (1992) on the Environment and Development was the second great international Conference after Stockholm Conference (1972) on Human Environment, where the largest number of States (200) which represented the world community gathered to study the problems of global environment over 20 years after Stockholm Conference. The Rio Conference has effected a magnificent result by achieving more understanding of the Members of international community on environmental cooperation and the conclusion of two important international Conventions on Biological Diversity and Climate Change.

Also the third important achievement of Rio Conference, besides the two international Conventions, was the Action Plan by UNCED on the global strategy of the environment and development for the coming 21 Century.

Agenda 21 is a multilateral and collective action addressed to the UN system, all States, other international organisations, NGOs and all groups, legal and natural persons, wherever they are at global level. So it involves all the international community. It is in fact, an international strategy for the protection of the environment and development put by the UN system for all the international community. It aims to benefit all peoples of the world, when care and enhancement of the environment will improve the economic development of all peoples, wherever they are, they will benefit from Agenda 21.

2. The EEC

Also the EEC for its part, has a good record in the environmental activities as a European regional organization.

The Maastricht Treaty (Art. 130r) has put the principal objectives of the EEC policies and actions concerning the environment, and called upon its Members to cooperate in achieving these objectives.

Moreover, the EEC in achieving its environmental policies has fully participated regionally and globally in negotiations for the consolidation and strengthening the international law of the environment and the conclusion of international conventions, either with the UN system or with other States and taking measures and the adoption of action programme and many Directives on the Environment.[3]

Also the role of other regional organizations, the SACEP, the OAU, OECD and many other

---

[1] - UNEP. UNEP Profile. Nairobi. 1990. PP 18-48.
[2] - Agora. Trade and Environment. AJIL. Vol.80. 1992. P.732.
[3] - Among the important Directives are:- (D.76/160 on Bathing Water), (D.76/46464 on Dangerous Substances), (D.80/68 on the Groundwater), (D.80/778 on Drinking Water), (D.91/271 on Urban Waste Water), (D.91/676 on Nitrate), (D.75/442 amended by 90/156 on Waste Framework), (D.78/319 amended by 689 on Hazardous Waste), (D.84/631 on Waste Movements), (Air Protection - D.80/779 on Sulphur), (D.85/203 on Nitrogen Dioxide), (D. on Ozone (1992), (D.82/884 on Lead in the Air). **DoE. The Environmental Policy of EEC.** 1992. pp. 4-9.

organizations (which have environmental activities), and NGO(s), are very effective in the protection of the global environment and enhancing the movement for global environment cooperation for the benefit of mankind.

B. The Universal Action

The universal action for the protection of environment is increasing its activities all over the world. This action is supporting the call for universal strategy on the one hand, and the international solidarity for the protection of the environment on the other.

The Green Movements all over the world are increasing their activities by creating great environmental groups for the adoption of environmental policies and actions and calling for popular participation at universal level for the protection of the environment and putting more pressure on States and governments all over the world to realize and fulfill their environmental programmes and policies and to strengthen the solidarity for global environmental protection. There is no doubt about the green strategy for the protection of the environment which has become a great mass movement at global level and involved a large number of societies all over the world.

The universal actions involve mass environmental movement which is supported by different groups of people, environmentalists, thinkers, writers, professors, teachers, farmers, workers and politicians who lead the universal actions for the protection of the earth and can coordinate the cooperation of peoples for better environment for them.

The universal actions are very necessary for the environmental policies, protection and the preservation of living and natural resources and for substantial development of all peoples. This necessity has its impact on the UNCED that called in its Agenda 21 upon major groups, women, youths and all communities at global level, local authorities, trade unions, businessmen, industrialists, scientists and technologists, that is all the world at large, to play their part in the environmental movement and actions.[1]

It is the global partnership, in universal action, which can effect great progress and results towards a better environment for all.

Section 3 - The Use of Technology

It becomes very necessary to use technology for the protection of the environment. The techological advance imposes a duty on the technological States and international community to use technology for the protection of the environment and to prevent harming it.

A. Exchange of Technological Information and Experience

The impact of technology on the environment is very strong, and the effect of human activities on the environment may cause damage to the environment as a consequence of the use of science and technology which can harm the environment.

Technology in the hand of humans has a double effect, it can do good and it can harm the environment and so it is the human's will which decides the right and good way to use technology for the environment.

Considering the important effect of technology on the environment the UNCED in Agenda 21

---

[1] - Global Partnership for Environment and Development. UNCED. Ibid. pp 94-104.

called upon the international community to make substantial efforts for the dissemination of sound and safe technologies.[1]

There is no doubt that the technological cooperation for the benefit of the environment which the Rio Summit (1992) addressed to the international community, it is the same problem which Agenda 21 deals with, is necessary for the protection of the global environment, it depends on the intentions and wills of the members of the international community, the degree of cooperation, the resources and the extent of the exchange of technological information.

But there are problems, regarding the exploitation of technologies for the benefit of the environment. These problems appear in States relations with each other. The degree of technological development, the difference in economic and industrial strata and the available technology for each State, community or society.

As concerns the global environment, the use of technology for the protection and enhancement of the environment necessitates the cooperation and partnership of all members of the international community which involves all the States and peoples of the world and this task cannot be performed unless each State and people cooperate and use its technical and scientific knowledge and experience for this purpose and by the collective cooperation, the global environment can be protected and enhanced for the interest of all the international community. The care and protection for the environment needs technology. For this purpose, all recent international environmental conventions addressed technology to their parties, and called upon them to cooperate in the exploitation of technology for the enhancement, protection and care for the environment and the exchange of technological data and experience.

The Maastricht Treaty in Art. 130r(3) has put the 'scientific and technical data' as one of the objectives of the EEC policy on environment. The exchange of technological information and experience is vital for the protection of the environment at a global level not only as it is the Community's objective in the cooperation among the Member-States. Besides, Art 16 of BDC (1992) has put the access to and the transfer of technology among the Contracting Parties as an objective of the Convention. The provision of this Article is broad in considering the necessity of broad cooperation among the Parties in all fields of technological advance and progress for the benefit of the environment.

Moreover, the CCC (Art. 9) addressed the use of technology in any study concerning the climate change and called upon the Parties to the Convention to cooperate fully by using their knowledge and technological experience and the exchange of technological data and information in this concern.

The Convention has well recognized the importance of establishing the (Subsidiary Body - organ) as a technical bank of data on climate change so that it can put the knowledge and experience at the disposal of all Parties.[2]

The UNCED has well addressed the importance of environmentally sound technologies which encompass total systems which include; 'know-how, procedures, goods and services and equipment as well as organizational and managerial procedures, human resource development, including gender considerations, and local capacity building are therefore relevant aspects of technology choices'.

Access to and transfer of these technologies and the capacity to develop and manage them are

---

[1] - UNCED. The Global Partnership. Ibid. p. 112.
[2] - See Art. of the Convention in the Annexes.

of particular importance to developing countries. Support should be provided to build the technological capacity of developing countries so that they can make more rational choices of technology relevant to their development.[1]

But the exchange of technological information and experience for the benefit of the developing countries, in order to protect the environment faces obstacles which the international economic order still imposes on the transfer of technology to the developing countries, and especially the existing protection of patents and intellectual property rights which do not permit the transfer of technology without the consent of the proprietor or the owner. This protection is becoming more stronger, when the industrial and developed countries insist on the protection in any negotiation or any new agreement. This is seen after the conclusion of the WTO agreement which will come into force by 1 January 1995.

This agreement has consolidated the protection of patents and intellectual property rights which form 80% of know-how, badly needed for the protection of the environment and have great impact on the international trade and development.

Moreover, the exchange of technological data and experience concerning the environment depends on the State's relations between each other, on the degree of technological development, whether the States have environmentally sound technologies.

Environmental technologies are very complicated and sophisticated and involve different know-how, some are very high, some are intermediate and others are primary technologies.

Environment is very large and broad, wide as our Mother Earth, it involves the atmosphere, the oceans, seas, the continents, the peoples (humans), animals and plants, the fauna and flora, the energy and natural resources. So the environment needs various technologies, including biotechnology. It is not easy for the international community to share as States differ in their technological develoment and advance. Some are rich (few) in technology, some are middle advanced and the large number of States are poor in technologies, they need to develop their resources in order to protect the environment and unless they have the sound available technologies they would stay poor and they cannot protect their environment.

So that the division between the rich and the poor countries will remain as it is, or may go worse, despite the purpose of the CCC and BDC to encourage the technological exchange of data and experience between States which depend largely on the ability to obtain patents and know-how which are subject to commercial exploitation and the ability to buy on the free market conditions. The poor countries cannot buy the environmental technologies in the free market. They have not the financial resources.

B - Exploiting the Technological Advance

Under the present International Economic Order, the poor countries cannot have the economic and financial resources to buy the environmental technologies. So the exploitation of technological advance remains with the reach of developed and industrial States which have the technological capabilities and resources to exploit and develop the environmental technologies for their own benefit and the protection of their environment. As concerns the global environment, there is need for cooperation between the developed and developing countries and this cooperation must not be just written on paper without any effect. Any cooperation needs a change in the conditions of exchange of environmental technologies which facilitate the transfer

---

[1] - UNCED. Global Partnership. Ibid. pp. 112-113.

Exploiting the Technological Advance

of technology; the patents and intellectual property rights which are still protected strongly by the last two international Conventions (CCC and BDC).

So exploiting the technological advance still be within the reach of the powerful technological States, which can use these technologies for the benefit of their environment, the developing countries cannot benefit from, unless adequate facilities and resources can be ensured for the least developed countries which need badly the transfer and access to technology for the purpose of BDC and CCC. Art. 16(2) of the BDC provides for effective protection of intellectual property rights. So the transfer of, and the access to, technology for the least developed countries depend on the financial resources which the Contracting Parties undertake to provide in accordance with Art. 20 of BDC,[1] while Art. 21 sets up the financial mechanism for providing the financial resources. Also Art. 11 of CCC sets up the financial Mechanism to provide for the essential resources for helping the developing countries to have access to technologies and can enhance its technological capabilities and so they can exploit for protection of the environment and can cooperate in the protection of the global environment with other States. So financial resources for the developing countries are very essential for the protection of global environment.

---

[1] - See Arts. (16-21) of the BDC and Art. 11 of the CCC in the Annexes.

Chapter 3

THE THREAT AGAINST THE ENVIRONMENT

Natural and human made disasters have always been threatening the environment, and cause concern about its dangers and its terrible consequences.
Although science and technology have revolutionized the means of protection of the environment, they have, at the same time, brought dangers and evil to it.
It is, as it is said in another place in this book, that science and technology are powers in the hands of humans, they can be used for good or evil. Regarding the threat, this Chapter involves three Sections: 1. Pollution, 2. Nuclear Tests, Explosion and Contamination, 3. Dumping.

Section 1 - Pollution

Within Chapter 2, Section 1, pollution under national law has been dealt with. The presentation is regarding the definition, description and the dangers pollution involves. In this place, the study concentrates on the legal dimensions and effects of international pollution.
In order to deal with pollution, under international law, it is necessary to present a framework of international conventions regarding pollution. International pollution has international effects which go beyond the jurisdiction of one State and so it affects another State or States or its dangers and damage affect the global environment.

A. Air Pollution

The most important international convention which protects the global environment from air pollution is the Geneva Convention of 13 November 1979 on 'Long Range Transboundary Air Pollution'.[1]

1. What is Air Pollution?

This Convention defines 'Air Pollution' (Art. 1) as the introduction by man, directly or indirectly, of substances or energy into the air resulting in deleterious effects of such a nature as to endanger human, harm living resources and ecosystems and material property and impair or interfere with amenities and other legitimate uses of the environment, and 'air pollutants' shall be construed accordingly.

2. Range of Air Pollution

Para. b) of the same Articles defines 'Long Range Transboundary Air Pollution' as 'pollution whose physical origin is situated wholly or in part within the area under national jurisdiction of one State and which has adverse effects in the area under the jurisdiction of another State at such a distance that it is not generally possible to distinguish the contribution of individual emission sources or groups or sources'.
The air pollution has a long range effect, it may affect the atmosphere, the ozone, the ecosystem and the global environment. Therefore it needs national and international measures to combat.
Air pollution can be natural without the interference of human or caused by pollutants introduced by human and contaminate the environment.[2]

---

[1] - See Kiss. Selected Multilateral Treaties in the Field of the Environment. UNEP Reference Series 3. UNEP 1882. p 519.

[2] - Art. 3 of the 'Long Range Transboundary Air Pollution' Convention.

Air Pollution

The effects of pollutants depend on their concentration.[3] If the level of emission is high, it would affect the human health and chronic sickness might occur.

3. Causes of Air Pollution

The causes of air pollution are many and the study of the physics of air pollution needs hundreds of pages, this book deals with the legal presentation of pollution, as causing damage to the environment. The atmospheric pollution is caused by the existence of pollutant gases more than the normal level. This usually happens by the increase of gases in the air. Air pollution affects the life, the health and the destruction of the ozone layer which protects the surface of the earth from the sunlight radiation.

i. The smoke

The increase of smoke (burning of fossil fuel, coal), oil, fire furnaces, factories, causes sulphur pollution (SO_2). Usually SO_2 causes SO_2 thick smoke in the atmosphere, when the air does not move. The increase of greenhouse gases in the atmosphere (especially CO_2) raises the temperature (one of the causes of climate change and the rise of the heat).[2]

ii. Acid Rain

Acid rain is another kind of air pollution and is caused by the increase of sulphur in the air, which pollutes the atmosphere. The increase of sulphur in the air in Western Europe causes acid rain which goes beyond the State territory and damages the forests and the green trees, especially in Scandinavia and Germany.

iii. Means of Transport

Means of transport (cars, vehicles, lorries) and other means of transport which use benzine and gasoline cause air pollution to a great extent that contaminates the environment and endangers the health and life.

The increase of emission of gases from oil causes dangerous air pollution. So many international conventions and declarations call upon the States and individuals to use less private transport means or use those which emit less gases in the air. Moreover, the Council of Europe (CoE) in its Res. No. (4) 68 of March 1968 called upon its Members to combat air pollution.[3]

iv. Photochemical Smog

In the last thirty years, this form of smog was known as a mixture of smog and fog including PAN (peroxyacyl nitrates), O_3 and NO_2. These gases become serious under sunshine and heat, when the pollutants are trapped and concentrated near the ground. The PAN is phytotoxic and an irritant to man at very low level (part per hundred million range), is produced mainly by the interaction of O_3, and unburned hydrocarbons.[4]

v. The Ozone

The Ozone as an oxygen based gas most of it, is the higher Ozone layer up to 20-30km above earth surface, which is the protector of the earth surface from sun beams radiation, as it works as barrier against ultra-violet rays (UVB), without it, the human and living organisms will be

---

[1] - Kenneth Mellanby. Ibid. p. 8.

[2] - DoE. Global Climate Change. 2nd Ed. p. 6.

[3] - In this Resolution the CoE warned of the harmful effects of air pollution and proposed the principles of prevention. 1. These differ according to the sources of pollution; 2. The industrial installations must not increase the air pollution and must be controlled by individual authorization, they must not emit pollutant gases in the air more than the accepted level; 3. Transport vehicles and cars must use oil and benzine of less emission of pollutant gases. **Kiss. La Protection Internationale de L'Environnement.** Ibid. pp. 37-38.

[4] - **Mellanby.** Ibid. p. 20.

under threat of death.[1]

The higher Ozone layer absorbs 49% of radiation from the sun's rays and prevents from reaching the earth. So the protection of the Ozone layer does a good function for protecting the human life and living organisms on earth.

The Vienna Convention for the Protection of the Ozone Layer of 22.3.1985 aims for the protection of human health and the environment against adverse effects resulting from modifications of the Ozone layer.[2]

Besides, the Montreal Protocol on Substances that Deplete the Ozone Layer of 16.9.1987 aims at the protection of the Ozone layer by taking precautionary measures to control global emissions of substances that deplete it.[3]

While the Amendment of this Protocl signed in London on 29.6.1990, provided for more control procedures in order to protect the Ozone Layer and to extend the coverage to new substances which deplete the Ozone layer. The Parties to the Convention agreed to reduce the emission of chlorofluorocarbons, carbon tetrachlorides and methyl chloroform in the air which were not covered by the first Protocol.[4]

The other kind of Ozone is lower Ozone which is near the earth, a greenhouse gas, it comes from the action of sunlight on vehicle exhaust gases. Low level ozone is a serious pollutant which causes respiratory and other health problems for many people.[5] The lower level ozone is smog dangerous to life, while the high level ozone is life saver.[6]

vi. Other Gases and Materials

Other gases such as carbon monoxide, carbon dioxide, methane and oxides of nitrogen pollute the air and cause threat to life and public safety.

Also materials like lead, zinc, copper and aluminium can react entirely with other materials that cause gases which pollute the air that can threathen health and public safety.

So it is necessary to keep watch on the use of dangerous materials which pollute the air in order to protect the environment.

4. International Meaures against Air Pollution

The measure for monitoring the quality of the protection of the atmosphere internationally have been under study and consideration during the last decade. The Global Environment Monitoring System (GEMS) has been monitoring the atmosphere and the air pollution in about 27-54 cities in the world, it gave results of its conclusion about the environmental development which can threaten the environment and cause atmospheric pollution, since 1979 after the conclusion of the Convention on Long Range Transboundary Air Pollution there has been constant monitoring of the emission of pollutants which cause air pollution of transboundary effects. Some of the conclusions of GEMS have been implemented by some countries (Germany, Sweden and another 12 countries in Western Europe). There is also an EEC Directive on the Reduction of the emission of gases that pollute the air by 50% of the level of 1980 by 2003.[7]

---

[1] - **Sainsbury's.** Pamphlet on the Environment. p. 6.
[2] - UNEP. Register of International Treaties and Other Agreements in the Field of the Environment. p. 208.
[3] - Ibid. p. 211.
[4] - Ibid. p. 214.
[5] - **Sainsbury's.** Ibid. p. 4.
[6] - Ibid.
[7] - **Kiss.** Ibid. pp. 35-36.

5. Duties of the Parties

The Convention binds the Parties under Arts. 3 and 4 to exchange information to make consultation and research and to monitor, develop without undue delay policies and strategies which shall serve as a means of combating the discharge of air pollutants, taking into account efforts already made at national and international levels, and must contribute to the reduction of air pollution including long-range transboundary air pollution.

6. EEC Directives

The EEC has introduced the system of preventive authorization regarding the atmospheric emission of gases from Industrial plants and factories. The Directive No. 84/360 Air Framwork Directive binds the Member-States to authorize previously the industrial plants and factories the level of emission of gases to the atmosphere, and the Member-States control any violation of the accepted level.

Moreover this Directive has put the principles of air pollution:
a. the use of most available technology to prevent air pollution;
b. respect for limit values of emission of gases;
c. the safeguard in each case of the standards of air pollution.[1]

Another important EEC Directive No. 80/779 on 'Sulphur' which sets up air quality standards which the Member-States must monitor the level of sulphur dioxide and smoke in the air and establish monitoring stations in zones of high pollution.[2]

Also the Lead in Air Directive No. 82/884 sets up the limits for lead concentrations and emissions (maximum 2 micrograms). The Member-States should impose disciplinary enforcement of the Directive regarding the persons who work in projects that use lead.[3]

B. Sea Pollution

Arts. 194-237 of the Convention on the Law of the Sea of (1982) have very well codified the necessary legal norms and obligations which are necessary to protect the marine environment. In Art. 194 particularly, the Conventions puts great responsibility on the Parties to take measures which prevent, reduce and control pollution of the marine environment.

The obligation to combat marine pollution from sources under State jurisdiction or the discharge of substances which cause the pollution.

The Conventions binds the States to harmonize their efforts in combating marine pollution.

The number of international conventions on sea pollution overrides any other international conventions on any other subjects. This expresses the alarm of the States and international community at the danger and threat of sea pollution to the marine environment and the marine living resources which must be protected on the one hand, and their importance as a source of human food on the other hand.

The great number of the Conventions on Sea Pollution increases the importance of the protection of seas against pollution and the call upon international community as a whole to cooperate for the protection of marine living resources. These Conventions add to the principles of International Law on pollution.

---

[1] - Kiss. Ibid. Luciano Butti. Emissioni Inquinanti in Atmosfera. Rivista Giuridica Dell' Ambiente. No. 5 Anno viii (1993).
[2] - DoE. Environment Protection in Europe. Ibid. p. 7.
[3] - Kiss. Ibid. pp. 36-37.

The Threat Against the Environment

Besides, a lot of international conventions deal with the sea pollution more than other kinds of pollution.[1]
The sea pollution is very dangerous and alarming as it causes great damage to the marine environment and the living resources, and its effects cannot easily prevented or taking the measures of protection against. The International Conventions warn the States to take the necessary measures to prevent the sea pollution from happening and to cooperate in meeting its dangerous effects.

1. Definition

The Kuwait Regional Convention for Cooperation on the Protection of the Marine Environment

---

[1] - **The International Conventions which are cited:-**
- The International Convention for the Prevention of Pollution of the Sea by Oil, signed in London on 12.5.1954 amended on 11 April 1962 and 21 October 1969 and 1971.
- Agreement for Cooperation in Dealing with Pollution of North Sea, signed in Bonn on 9.6.1969.
- Convention relating to International Intervention on the High Seas in cases of Oil Pollution Casualties, signed in Brussels on 29 November 1969.
- International Convention on Civil Liability for Oil Pollution Damage, signed in Brussels on 29.9.1969.
- International Convention on the Establishment of an International Fund for Compensation for Oil Pollution Damage, signed in Brussels in 1969 amended on 18 December 1971.
- International Convention for the Prevention of Pollution from Ships, signed in London on 2 November 1973.
- Protocol of 1978 relating to the International Convention for the Prevention of Pollution from Ships (1973), signed in London 1978.
- Protocol Relating to Intervention on the High Seas in Cases of Marine Pollution by Substances other than Oil, signed in London on 2 November 1977.
- Convention on the Protection of Marine Environment of the Baltic Sea Area, signed in Helsinki on 22 March 1974.
Convention for the Prevention of Marine Pollution from Land-Based Sources, signed in Paris on 4 June 1974.
- Procotol Protecting the Mediterranean Sea against Pollution, signed in Barcelona on 16 February 1979.
- Protocol concerning Cooperation in Combating Pollution of the Mediterranean Sea by Oil and other Harmful Substances in Cases of Emergency, signed in Barcelona on 2 February 1971.
- International Convention on Civil Liability for Oil Pollution Damage, signed in Brussels on 29 November 1969, amended in 1981.
- Convention on the Prohibition of Military or any other Hostile use of Environmental Modification Techniques, signed in Geneva on 18 May 1977.
- Kuwait Regional Convention for the Protection of Marine Environment Against Pollution, signed in Kuwait on 23.4.1978.
- Convention for the Protection of the Marine Environment and Coastal Area of South-East Pacific, signed in Lima on 12.11.1981.
- Protocol Concerning Cooperation in Combating Pollution in Cases of Emergency, signed in Abidjan on 23.3.1981.
- Agreement on Regional Cooperation in Combating Pollution of the South-East Pacific by Oil or Other Harmful Substances in Cases of Emergency, signed in Lima on 12.11.1981.
- Supplementary Protocol to the Agreement on Regional Cooperation in Combating Pollution of South-East Pacific by Oil and other Harmful Substances in Cases of Emergency, signed in Quito on 22.7.1983.
- Protocol Concerning Regional Cooperation in Combating Pollution by Oil and other Harmful Substances in Cases of Emergnecy, signed in Jidda on 15.2.1982.
- Convention for the Protection and Development of the Marine Environment of the Wider Caribbean Region, signed in Cartagena on 24.3.1983.
- Protocol Concerning Cooperation in Combating Oil Spills in the Wider Caribbean Region, signed in Cartagena on 24.3.1983.
- Agreement for Cooperation in Dealing wiht Pollution of the North Sea by Oil and other Harmful Substances, signed in Bonn on 13.9.1983.
- Convention for the Protection, Management and Development of the Marine and Coastal Environment of the Eastern African Region, signed in Nairobi on 21.6.1985.
- Protocol Concerning Cooperation in Combating Marine Pollution in Cases of Emergency in the Eastern African Region, signed in Nairobi on 21.6.85.

from Pollution[1] defines 'Marine Pollution' as the introduction by man, directly or indirectly, of substances or energy into the marine environment resulting or likely to result in such deleterious effects as harmful to living resources, hazards to human health, hindrance to marine activities including fishing, impairment of quality for use of sea and reduction of amenities.

It seems from this definition that the Convention regards marine pollution is caused directly or indirectly by human, it excludes the pollution which happens by natural causes or disasters as ocean or sea volcanoes which erupt and pollute the environment and cause the death of the marine living resources or diseases which kill the fauna and flora. So the natural pollution is not covered by the Convention.

2. What Causes Sea Pollution?

The Law of the Sea's Convention which deals with sea pollution has related the causes of marine pollution to oil carried by ships, dumping of waste, hazardous substances (toxic, harmful, noxious sewage by ships, land-based sources Art. 194/3a Law of the Sea) or from or through the atmosphere (Art. 194/aii).

3. The Law of Sea Pollution

The Convention on the Law of the Sea (Arts. 194-237) has provided for the general principles of the law of sea pollution. These principles have been reasserted in the many international conventions on marine pollution or the protection of the marine environment in one way or the other and set up the particular rules and obligations of the parties to the conventions.

a. The General Principles

The General Principles of the law of sea pollution have been set up by the Convention on the Law of the Sea which imposes a duty on the State to prevent sea pollution, to protect the marine environment and therefore, they acknowledge the right of the State to exploit the marine resources without causing damage to the marine environment (Art. 194).

Also the law of the sea obligates the State to take the necessary measures to prevent, reduce, control the pollution of the marine environment (Art. 194).

Also States, when exercising their activities within their jurisdiction must not cause damage by pollution to other States or to their environment and not allow pollution under their control to go beyond the areas where they exercise sovereign rights in accordance with the law.

Also the law of the sea imposed a duty on the State to cooperate with other States regionally or with the international community globally, to control, prevent sea pollution and to use the necessary technology under its disposal for this purposes.

These are the main principles adopted by the Convention on the Law of the Sea.

b. The Particular Principles

All the international conventions and protocols on the sea pollution and the protection of the marine environment assert the general principles adopted by the Convention on the Law of the Sea, but at the same time they set up particular principles which relate to the specific function and purposes of each of them. These particular principles can be summarized in order to facilitate their study.

i. The Biding Effects

Each of the conventions or protocols binds the States parties to them in particular obligations.

---

[1] - **Kiss. Selected Multilateral Treaties in the Field of the Environment.** Ibid. UNEP. p. 486 and also the Convention for the Protection of Marine Environment in the Baltic Sea Area, Ibid. p. 405.

The Threat Against the Environment

ii. The Territoriality

Every one of the conventions or protocols has been concluded to govern a particular region or area in its implementation.

iii. The Principle of Cooperation

Each of the Conventions or Protocols calls upon the State's cooperation by taking measures, adopts rules, laws or other measures, for the implementation of the convention or the protocol.

iv. Setting up Fund or Centre

Some of the Conventions sets up Fund or Centre for the control of the implementation of the convention or the realization of the financial resources.

v. Regulations for the Navigation of Ships and Carriage of Oil

The Conventions or Protocols which deal with the carriage of oil or harmful substances set up the regulations of the navigation of ships and the carriage of oil or harmful substances.

vi. The Emergencies

The particularity of the State's obligation to deal with the emergencies of marine pollution when they threaten the Member-States, other States, the marine environment, so that the State is bound to take the necessary measures to protect the marine environment, to inform other States or to request for their cooperation and assistance as necessary, or through the emergency mutual aid or fund or centre.

vii. Using Technology and Scientific Research

Many of the conventions call upon the States to use technology and the scientific research in order to combat the pollution of the marine environment and exchange information with the other Parties for the protection of the international marine environment and the need of the collective efforts of all the international community.

4. The Protection of the Marine Living Resources

Sea pollution is a great threat and danger to the marine living resources, as has been explained in the study of the conventions on sea pollution and the protection of the marine environment, the international community is very worried about the enormous loss of the marine living resources by sea pollution by ships, oil and other harmful substances and from coastal sources that cause sea pollution and kill the living resources or the global fisheries which are great food sources which feed millions of people all over the world, especially poor countries in Africa.

So to combat pollution of the sea and to control or to prevent, it is a great task on the shoulders of the international community to cooperate in order to protect the marine environment and its resources.

C. Land Pollution and its Causes

Land pollution is also very dangerous and alarming as air and sea pollution. Moreover land pollution affects the health and public safety and the living resources; animals, plants and is more destructive to the economy, development and welfare.

The effects of land pollution are seen to be more destructive in the developing countries and the Third World, where they have not the technology and financial resources to combat land pollution and to protect their environment and to take the preventive measures to minimize its dangers or to deal with its effects when it happens.

Land pollution affects the fauna and flora and the ecosystem, human health and puts pressures on the State's economy and its development.

Moreover, the Third World faces the effects of land pollution which hinders its development and especially, the sound sustainable development it needs badly which Agenda 21 calls upon the States to achieve in order to strengthen the global economic advance for all peoples.

Land pollution destroys the natural environment and causes damage to human health and safety and the living resources, humans, animals and plants and harms the natural habitat. Land pollution affect other States when goes beyond a state's jurisdiction, it will have international effects.

Agenga 21 warns against the menace of urban pollution which damages the urban life as an effect of industrial pollution.

Land pollution is the most damageable to human and natural environment, because the land is the natural environment of the most biological species whether humans or the fauna or flora. So the protection of the environment needs to study its causes in order to take preventive measures to prevent the pollution and its harmful effects.

The causes of land pollution are:

a. **Urban Life (particularly populated and industrialized cities)**

The urban life has become one of the most dangerous causes of land pollution because of the by-product of industrial processes which pollute the environment.[1]

Urban pollution exists on a great scale in the Third World, an example of industrial pollution is the Bhopal disaster in 1984 in India, where hundreds of thousands of people were affected by this disaster.

Moreover, urban areas dispose of large amounts of contaminants derived from litter, garbage, carwashings, horticultural treatments, vehicle drippings, industry construction, animal droppings and the chemicals used for snow and ice clearance and domestic sewage.[2]

Besides land pollution, urban and industrialized cities pollute the rivers and air with great harm to the environment, especially when no preventive measures are taken to reduce its effects.

b. **Waste**

The disposal of waste in large quantities pollute the land, especially waste landfill sites. The discharge of waste in landfill sites creates methane as a result of the action of bacteria on organic waste which pollutes the air also.[3] The EECC has proposed for the amendment of the Directive on the Landfill Waste, the aim of the amendment is to harmonise technical standards for waste disposal in landfill sites. The Commission in its proposal rejects the banning of disposal of liquid waste in landfill sites, but the Member-States must provide annual reports about landfill sites and detailed facts about waste.[4]

The Basel Convention on the Control of Transboundary Movements of Hazardous Wastes and their Disposal, signed in Basel on 22.3.1989 has set up obligations on the Parties to reduce the movements of transboundary waste movements with a view to minimize the danger of pollution of the environment of the Member-States and ensuring good management which protects the environment. The Convention prohibits the import of hazardous waste or other wastes and calls upon the Parties to inform the Signatories of their decision according to Art. 13. The Parties shall prohibit and not permit the export of hazardous wastes to the Parties who have prohibited the import of such wastes (Art. 4(1a)). The Convention binds the Parties to respect the restrictions on the movement of wastes whether the import or export exercised by the Parties or the individuals, the Parties should prohibit their subjects or persons under their jurisdiction from transporting or disposing of hazardous wastes unless they are authorized.

The Convention calls upon the Parties to cooperate in implementing the Convention in order to

---

[1] - W M Adams. Green Development. Routledge. 1992. p. 114.
[2] - Andrew Goudie. **The Human Impact on the Natural Environment.** Blackwell. 4th Ed. 1993. p. 222.
[3] - Sainsbury's. Ibid.
[4] - European Information Service. No. 141 (93).

The Threat Against the Environment

achieve a sound environmental management of hazardous wastes. Any Parties should inform the other Parties about accidents during the movement of wastes immediately.[1]

c. Chemical, Toxic Pollutants and Insecticides

Chemicals, toxic pollutants and insecticides or pesticides create land pollution. DDD, DDE, DDT, when highly concentrated, threaten the wildlife, not only insects and larvae, but animals and sea birds. They pollute the land, the rivers and contaminate the environment. Farmers should be cautious about the use of insecticides in agriculture, as DDT, organo-chlorine, organo-phosphorus, carbonate which may be useful prima facie to agriculture, but later or in the long run, their concentration spreads rapidly to surroundings and could pollute the land and rivers.[2] Nevertheless, although WHO can present a good advice about the use of DDT against malaria, but it may pollute the land and kill animals and birds.

FAO and UNEP have established Cooperative Programme on Integrated Pest Control in South East Asia tackling this problem and tried to reduce the level of the use of pesticides and the exercise of control.[3]

Moreover, pesticides create also another problem of hazardous waste disposal especially when they are concentrated and go beyond their intended areas, and if the problem becomes so serious, it leads to intensive environmental pollution and the possibility of the rise of death.

The industrial and developed countries are capable of controlling the use of pesticides in agriculture, but the trade with the Third World in pesticides may lead to use them extensively in agriculture and would create environmental pollution.

The European Agreement on the Restriction of the Use of Certain Detergents in Washing and Cleaning Products, signed in Strasbourg on 16.9.1968 restricts the use and sale of cleaning products unless they satisfy certain conditions which protect the environment and contribute to human well being.[4]

d. Bad Agriculture

Bad agriculture pollutes the land and damages its productivity and may affect the growth of other plants and spreads diseases.

Farmers are usually the real cause of bad agriculture, when they ignore the modern means of cultivation and farming, they do not use good means of drainage where the water remains over the land and become stagnant and the land becomes swampy that produces plant diseases.

---

[1] - UNEP. Register of Treaties.
[2] - **Goudie**. Ibid. p. 119.
[3] - Ibid. p. 119.
[4] - Other Conventions cited are:
- International Convention on the Prohibition of the Development, Production and Stockpiling of Baceteriological (Biological) and Toxic Weapons and on Their Destruction, signed in London, Moscow and Washington on 10.11.72. These weapons pollute the environment and are dangerous to the fauna and flora.
- Convention on the Conservation of the European Wildlife and Habitat, signed in Berne on 19.9.1979.
- Benelux Convention on Nature Conservation and Landscape Protection, signed in Brussels on 8.6.1982.
- Protocol Concerning Protected Areas and Wild Fauna and Flora in the Eastern African Region, signed in Nairobi on 21.6.85.
- Asian Agreement on the Conservation of Nature and Natural Resources, signed in Kuala Lumpur on 9.7.85.
- Convention on the Protection of Natural Resources and Environment of the South-Pacific Region, signed in Noumea on 24.11.86
- Protocol Concerning Cooperation in Combating Pollution Emergencies in the South-Pacific Region signed in Noumea on 25.11.86

So bad agriculture does not only cause pollution of the land but also would damage the land productivity and become dangerous to the health and the fauna and the flora.

e. Mining and the Coal Industry

Mining and Coal Industry cause land pollution by damaging its productivity and killing the fauna and flora in the areas which minerals and oil affect the soil components and may create toxic waste which kills the wildlife.

Section 2 - Nuclear Tests, Explosion and Contamination

The development of the use of nuclear power for peaceful purposes, although it is a great achievement of science and technology, but the development of nuclear power, whether for peace or war creates a great threat to the environment. The nuclear tests, explosion and contamination create radioactivity which threatens the environment by radiation that endangers the human life and the living resources.

In this Section, it is necessary to deal with:

A - Nuclear Radiation in the Atmosphere

Nuclear radiation in the atmosphere is caused by the nuclear reactors which produce nuclear energy as the Nuclear Station explosion of Chernobyl in 1986 which produced nuclear clouds that polluted the atmosphere of several Western Countries, it released 40% of its radioactive materials in the atmosphere.[1]

1. Radioactive Materials

Radiation is the emission of radio waves, micro waves, visible light, X-rays, gamma rays and laser.[2]

Radiation is the transmission of a form of energy by electromagnetic waves. Electromagnetic radiation is sending particles (photons) accompanied by waves, they differ in the amount of energy they possess.[3]

The materials which have radioativity are the main source of nuclear energy are: uranium, protactinium and thorium. These naturally occuring heavy elements have a nucleus which is unstable and tends to break apart comparatively easily.[4]

2. The Control of and Protection Against Radioactivity

The radioactivity can be useful for medical purposes, as controlled X-rays, or for cancer treatment, but at the same time, it can be dangerous, if the body or the living organ is exposed for a long time, and more than the accepted level.

It is believed that Radon is one of the dangerous elements which causes lung cancer. Radon is a gas emitted by Radium and Uranium, the two radioactive elements.

As a matter of fact, the production of nuclear energy would be safe, if there were tight control of the production processes. The danger comes of the fission (break apart) of the nuclei of heavy radioactive elements which produces extra high heat which causes great explosion if it is not controlled in a counted degree. Big nuclear explosion causes nuclear atmospheric pollution

---

[1] - Graham Maclachen. A Green Alamanc. Lochar Publishers Ltd. 1991. p. 113.
[2] - Steven Elsworth. A Dictionary of the Environment. Paladium. 1990. p. 375.
[3] - Herman & Leo Schneider. Dictionary of Science for Everyone. Paragon Books. 1993. p. 239.
[4] - Dictionary for Science for Everyone. Ibid.

and radioactive clouds which are dangerous to the global environment and threaten all humans and the living resources (animals and plants).

In order to protect the environment from the nuclear pollution it is necessary to set up safety systems which have tight control on the nuclear installations and the transport of fissile materials.[1]

3. Nuclear Tests and Explosion in the Atmosphere

Nuclear tests and explosion are dangerous to the environment, because nuclear radioactivities pollute the atmosphere.

Generally spearking, any use of nuclear energy, even for peaceful purposes may create danger of explosion that causes radioactivity of fissile materials and radioactive wastes which pollute the atmosphere, especially in the absence of tight and safe control.[2]

i. The Treaty on Banning Nuclear Weapons Tests and Explosion

But the tests and explosion of nuclear weapons is more worrying and dangerous to the environment than the use of nuclear energy for peaceful purposes. For the purpose of protection of the environment and humankind, the banning of nuclear weapons tests in the atmosphere and outer space is envisaged in the Treaty on Banning Nuclear Weapon Tests in the Atmosphere, in Outer Space and Under Water, signed in Moscow on 5.8.1963.[3]

This Treaty has put obligation on the Parties in order to 'prevent, and not carry out any nuclear weapon test explosion, other nuclear explosion, at any place under its jurisdiction or control.' Art.1.(1).

a) in the atmosphere, beyond its limits, including outer space; or under water, including territorial waters or high seas; or

b) in any other environment if such explosion causes radioactive debris to be present outside the territorial limits of the State under whose jurisdiction or control such explosion is conducted. It is understood in this connection that the provision of this sub-paragraph are without prejudice to the conclusion of a treaty resulting in the permanent banning of all nuclear test explosions, including all such explosions underground, the conclusion of which, as the Parties have stated in the preamble of this Treaty they seek to achieve' Art.1(1b).

While Para. (2) of Art.1 binds the Parties to refrain from causing, encouraging or in any way participating in, the carrying out of any nuclear test explosion, or any other nuclear explosion, anywhere which would take place in any of the environment described, or have the effect referred to, in paragraph 1 of the same Article.

ii. Protection of the Outer Space against Contamination

The Treaty on the Principles Governing the Activities of States in the Exploration and Use of Outer Space Including the Moon and Other Celestial Bodies has established the legal regime for the exploration and use of outer space. It binds the Parties to refrain from placing objects carrying nuclear weapons of mass destruction in outer space, and shall use the Moon and other celestial bodies exclusively for peaceful purposes (Art.VII).

Also the Parties should avoid harmful contamination of the outer space and adverse changes in

---

[1] - The ECJ judgment of 11 February 1992 in the Case No. 308/90, Advanced Nuclear Fuels GmbH v EC, the Court said, "The provisions of EAEC Treaty which sought to prevent the diversion of nuclear materials from their intended uses were fundamental to the attainment of the tasks of Euratrom therefore any failure to observe these rules constituted a serious infringement". TLR 11.2.92.

[2] - Nuclear Fission Safety. EEC Official Journal L. 336 of 7.12.1991.

[3] - **Kiss. (UNEP) Selected Multilateral Treaties.** Ibid. p. 185.

the environment of the Earth resulting from the introduction of extra-terrestrial matter (Art.IX). The Treaty has put international responsibility on the Parties for their national activities in outer space and would be responsible for the damage they cause to other Parties (Art.VIII).
So this Treaty regards the internal activities of the States in violation of the Treaty come under international law as the environment is a global concern. It concerns the common interest of humankind.

iii. Preventing the Spread of Nuclear Weapons and Protection Against the Danger of Nuclear War

A further advance of the UN efforts for preventing the danger of spread of Nuclear Weapons and the pursuit of complete disarmament, the Treaty on the Non-Proliferation of Nuclear Weapons had been adopted by the GA on 12 June 1968. In the preamble of the Treaty the UN has stressed the importance of the protection of mankind from the danger of nuclear war and to ensure the measures of safeguarding the security of all peoples and the prevention of the dissemination of nuclear weapons which pollute the environment.

Art.1 of the Treaty binds the Parties not to transfer to any recipient whatsoever nuclear weapons or other nuclear explosive devices or control over such weapons or explosive devices directly, or indirectly; and not in any way to assist, encourage, or induce any non nuclear weapon State to manufacture or otherwise acquire nuclear weapons or other nuclear devices, or control over such weapons or explosive devices.

Art.2 of the Treaty binds the Parties not to receive the transfer from any transferer whatsoever of nuclear weapons or other nuclear explosive device or of control over such weapons or explosive directly, or indirectly; not to manufacture or otherwise acquire nuclear weapons or other nuclear explosive devices; and not to seek or receive anay assistance in the manufacture of nuclear weapons or other nuclear explosive devices.

Arts.III, IV and V of the Treaty involve safeguards for the implementation of the Treaty, the role of the International Atomic Energy Agency in the inspection and verification system and the cooperation of the Parties with this Agency and other technical matters concerning the use or the production of special fissionable matter subject to the Treaty and the development of the Parties' capabilities technologically for the use of atomic energy for peaceful purposes which the Treaty does not prevent and the cooperation of the Parties in getting benefits from research and development of the peaceful use of atomic science.[1] The Treaty on the Non-Proliferation of Nuclear Weapons has a very important task which is the protection of the atmosphere from nuclear explosion which pullutes the atmosphere and creates nuclear clouds.[2]

4. Contamination of the Atmosphere

Contamination of the atmosphere is caused by:

i. The Nuclear Wastes

The nuclear wastes which are produced by the processes of nuclear energy are very dangerous to the environment and the atmosphere. The radioactivity of the nuclear waste contaminates the atmosphere, especially, when the nuclear wastes are ejected in the outer space, or the wastes are left on the ground or in surface storage without safety or control, where high level active nuclear waste emits dangerous radiation into the atmosphere.

The nuclear clouds in the atmosphere affect the Earth and cause damage to the ecology, habitats,

---

[1] - Kiss. Says security and control do not prevent the peaceful nuclear development. Ibid. p. 53.
[2] - France joined the Treaty (NPT) formally, and became party to the Treaty. Its Parties are 151. The Irish Times. 5 August 1992.

human health and the living resources.[1]

ii. Greenhouse Gases Emission

The increase of the emission of the greenhouse gases, CFCs, CO_2, Nitrous Oxide, Halocarbons and Methane contaminates the atmosphere and endangers the Ozone layer.
The great danger comes from the depletion of the Ozone layer which is caused by halocarbones. The Ozone layer protects the Earth from sun radiation and increased heat.
Also the increase of greenhouse gases in the atmosphere causes climate change and warm weather which affects the global climate.
Greenhouse gases are emitted through energy conversion, as well as through industrial and agricultural activities. Local and transboundary pollution originated from the combustion of fossil and biomass fuels, which affects the green of the Earth and health of population. The increase of radiation, especially ultraviolet radiation, reaching the Earth's surface affects seriously human health and increases skin cancer and eye disease. The CCC task is to find the international legal solution by demanding more cooperation of States and all Members of the International community and using more financial resources and technology to meet the need of dealing with the effects and causes of climate change.[2]

B. Explosion in the Sea Bed

Nuclear explosion in the sea bed is very dangerous as it pollutes and contaminates the sea bed and ocean floor and affects long and wide areas of the sea water with the danger of spreading to a far and long distance that threatens the marine living resources and environment.
Two treaties have dealt with nuclear explosion in the sea bed and ocean floor.
The first is the **Treaty on Banning Nuclear Weapon Tests in the Atmosphere, in Outer Space and Under Water.** This Treaty has been explained as regards the atmosphere and outer space. But now it is necessary to deal with what concerns the sea bed. (Under Water).
The Second Treaty is the **Treaty on the Prohibition of the Emplacement of Nuclear Weapons and Other Weapons of Mass Destruction on the Sea-Bed and Ocean Floor and the Subsoil Thereof.**

1. **The Treaty on Banning Nuclear Weapons Test in the Atmosphere, in Outer Space and Under Water** signed in Moscow on 5 August 1963 whose initiators are the three big atomic weapons producers, UK, USA and USSR (Russia) as original Parties of the Treaty stated in the preamble of the Treaty "Their aim is the speediest possible achievement of an agreement on general and complete disarmament under strict international control in accordance with the objectives of the UN which would put an end to the armament race and eliminate the incentive to the production and testing of all kinds of weapons, including nuclear weapons".[3] This binding declaration in the Treaty by the Parties is very important and effective indeed, because it satisfies the wishes of all peoples of the world and if the nuclear race ends it will be a new epoch for the protection of humankind from the danger of nuclear weapons.[4]

---

[1] - Kiss. Ibid. p. 53.
[2] - UNCED. The Global Partnership, Guide to Agenda 21. Ibid. p 74.
[3] - Kiss. (UNEP). Multilateral Treaties. Ibid. p 185.
[4] - President Yeltsin's proposal in his speech on 26.9.94 in UNGA for treaty on Nuclear Security and Strategic stability involves the five Nuclear Powers China, France, Russia, UK and US is a step forward for complete disarmament and the protection of the global environment from Nuclear weapons' threat.

Accidents in Nuclear Energy Plants

The Treaty in Art. 1(a) binds the Parties not to carry out any nuclear weapons test explosion at .... or 'under water, including territorial waters or high seas'.
While Para. 2 of the same Article provides that the Parties in this Treaty undertake furthermore to refrain from causing, encouraging or in any way participating in, the carrying out of any nuclear weapon test explosion, anywhere which would take place in any of the environment described or have the effect referred to, in Paragraph 1 of this Article.
This is a good treaty for nuclear safety of the sea-bed and under water of the territorial and high seas and protects the marine living resources and the environment from contamination. But it needs to be accepted by other nuclear powres as France and China and other States which aim to be nuclear weapons producers and working to achieve their aims. May this Treaty give them an opportunity to join in good faith and to refrain from the attempts of producing nuclear weapons.
2. **The Treaty on the Prohibition of the Emplacement of Nuclear Weapons and Other Weapons of Mass Destruction on the Sea-Bed and Ocean Floor and in the Subsoil thereof.**
This Treaty which was signed in London, Moscow and Washington on 11th February 1971 is another step forward for the protection of the sea-bed, ocean floor and subsoil thereof, from the danger of nuclear weapons that threaten the marine environment and its living resources.
Once more the Original Parties stated in the preamble of the Treaty that it constitutes a step towards a general and complete disarmament under strict and effective international control.
Of course the prohibition of the emplacement of nuclear weapons on the sea bed, the ocean floor and subsoil means a guarantee for safety of marine environment and the protection of the sea-bed from nuclear explosion and ensuring the exploitation of the high seas for peaceful purposes.
Art.1 of the Treaty binds the Parties not to emplant and emplace nuclear weapons on the sea-bed and ocean floor and in the subsoil thereof beyond the outer limit of a sea-bed zone as defined in Art.(II) any nuclear weapons or any other types of weapons of mass destruction as well as structures, launching installations or any other facilities specifically designed for storing, testing or using such weapons.
This provision is a good guarantee for the protection of the sea-bed from the nuclear explosion as it prohibits the emplacement and the use of nuclear weapons on the sea-bed, ocean floor and in the subsoil and so there would not be any attempt to explode nuclear weapons under water in the high seas and oceans, including limits of territorial sea and contiguous zone provided in Art.II of the Treaty. The nuclear explosion or any explosion tests would contaminate the waters of the high sea and ocean and endanger the marine living resources and the environment that the Treaty protects and prevents the mass destruction of the environment.

C. Accidents in Nuclear Energy Plants and of Nuclear Weapons.

Accidents in nuclear plants and of nuclear weapons cause worries and fear of the danger of nuclear contamination and radiation which cause great danger to the environment, atmosphere and the human health and safety. Nuclear accidents have great impact on national and international law and so, both insist on the safety and control on the nuclear plants and the transport of nuclear materials and weapons.
Regarding international law of the environment, the protection against nuclear accidents and the compensation of the victims, many international norms have been developed in the last two decades.

The Threat Against the Environment

In this respect there are certain international conventions[1], which put obligations on the Parties in order to deal with the accidents or to compensate the victims.

1. The Convention on Early Notification of a Nuclear Accident

This Convention was signed in Vienna on 26.9.86. Its objectives are to bind the Parties to notify directly or through the International Atomic Energy Agency, any Party affected by the accident in order to take the necessary measures to meet the consequences of the effects of the nuclear accident and to cooperate with the other Parties for ensuring the nuclear safety[2] or to stop or to prevent its damage and contamination effects.

The Convention binds the Parties to give full information of the accident and its radiological effects on transboundary environment in order to limit its effects.

Art.1 of the Convention provides for the field of application.[3]

1. The present Convention applies to every accident which relates to installations or activities enumerated in the following Para.2 of the State Party or natural or legal persons under its jurisdiction or under its control who involve or shall involve in radioactive waste and which would be consequently a transboundary international waste capable to affect the radiological safety of another State.

2. The installations or the activities intended in Para.1 are the following:-
a) any nuclear reactor wherever is situated;
b) any installation of nuclear fuel;
c) any installation involves in the management of radioactive waste,
d) the transport or the storage of nuclear fuel or radioactive waste;
e) the temporary production, use, storage or permanent storage and the transport of radio-isotopes for agricultural or industrial and medical purposes and for scientific connections or research;
f) the use of radio-isotopes for the production of electricity in space objects.

Art.3 of the same Convention provides that the States Parties can notify the other Parties in any nuclear accident which does not come under the provision of Article 1.[4]

2. The Convention on Assistance in the Case of a Nuclear Accident or Radiological Emergency.

This Convention which was signed in Vienna on 26.9.86 provides for the cooperation of its Parties among themselves and with the International Atomic Energy Agency to facilitate the prompt assistance in the event of nuclear accident or radiological emergency.

The Convention gives the International Atomic Energy Agency an important role to assist the Parties when a nuclear accident happens and they request its assistance.

---

[1] - The Conventions cited are:
- Convention on Third Party Liability in the Field of Nuclear Energy, signed in Paris on 29.7.1960, amended on 28.1.64, 16.11.82 and 1.4.68.
- Convention Supplementary to the Paris Convention of 29 July 1960, signed in Brussels on 31 January 1963.
- Vienna Convention on Civil Liabiity for Nuclear Damage, signed in Vienna on 21 May 1963.
- Convention Relating to Civil Liability in the Field of Maritime Carriage of Nuclear Material, signed in Brussels on 17.12.1971.
- Convention on the Physical Protection of Nuclear Material, signed in Vienna and New York on 3.3.1980.
- Convention on Assistance in the Case of Nuclear Accident or Radiological Emergency, signed in Vienna on 26.9.86.
- Convention on Early Notification of a Nuclear Accident, signed in Vienna on 26.9.86.

[2] - Kiss. Ibid. p. 54.
[3] - Ibid.
[4] - Ibid.

Liability for Nuclear Damage

According to Art.2 if a Party needs assistance in the event of a nuclear accident or radiological emergency, whether or not such accident or emergency originatnes within its territory, jurisdiction or control, it may call for such assistance from any other State Party, directly or through the Agency, and from the Agency, or where appropriate, from other international intergovernmental organizations.

3. Protection of Nuclear Material Against Accidents

The Convention on the Physical Protection of Nuclear Material, signed in Vienna and New York on 3.3.1980 provided for the safety of nuclear material and the effective measures of its protection during its transport within the territory of the Parties or on board of the ship or aircraft under their jurisdiction.

The Convention binds the Parties not to export nuclear material unless they have received assurances that such material will be protected during its internatonal transport.[1]

And Art.4(3) does not allow the transit of their territories by land or internal waterways or through their airports or seaports of nuclear material between States that are not parties to this Convention unless they have received assurances that this nuclear material will be protected during international nuclear transport.[2]

4. Liability for Nuclear Damage

There are five international conventions involving the liability of nuclear damage; the first is the Paris Convention on Third Party Liability in the Field of Nuclear Energy of 29 July 1960[3], the second is the Brussels Convention Supplementary to the Paris Convention (which is mentioned above), of 31 January 1963[4]; the third is the Vienna Convention on Civil Liability for Nuclear Damage of 21 May 1963[5]; the fourth is the Brussels Convention Relating to Civil Liability in the Field of Maritime Carriage of Nuclear Material of 17 December 1971[6] and the fifth is the Joint Protocol Relating to the Application of the Vienna Convention and the Paris Convention.[7]

These Conventions are very important regarding the liability for nuclear damage, and when an action for compensation would be raised, it is necessary to consider them all together, in order to make the action successful, and not to be confused with which one of them to be applied.

i. **Principles of Liability**
a. **Relating to Installation**

The operator of the nuclear installation[8] is liable for the damage caused by nuclear

---

[1] - UNEP. **Register of International Treaties**. Ibid. p. 161.
[2] - Ibid. p. 161.
[3] - **Kiss (UNEP)**. Ibid. p. 159.
[4] - Ibid. p. 171.
[5] - Ibid. p. 179.
[6] - Ibid. pp. 253-255.
[7] - This Protocol establishes a link between the two Conventions and eliminates the conflicts arising from the stimulous application of both to a nuclear accident. Each Convention applies to each incident to the exclusion of the other. Moreover, according to the Protocol, Arts. I-XV of the Vienna Convention are applied to the Parties of the Protocol that are Parties to the Paris Convention. Arts. 1-14 of the Paris Convention are applied to the Parties of the Protocol that are Parties to the Vienna Convention. UNEP **Register of International Treatie.s** Ibid. p. 242.
[8] - The Nuclear Installation according to the amended Paris Convention is reactors other than those comprised in any means of transport; factories for the manufacture or processing of nuclear substances; factories for separation of isotopes of nuclear fuel, factories for the reprocessing of irradiated nuclear fuel; facilities for the storage of nuclear substances other than storage incidental to the carriage of such substances; and such other installations in which there are nuclear fuel or radioactive products or waste as the Steering Committee of the European Nuclear Agency shall from time to time determine.

The Threat Against the Environment

incident.[1]

This liability involves:
1) loss of life or any person;
2) loss of property, other than the nuclear installation itself and any property on the site of that installation which is used or to be used in connection with that installation (Art 3(a) of the amended Paris Convention.

b. Regarding the Nuclear Material

The operator is also liable for the damage caused by incident of nuclear material or substance, whether it is in the installation or in temporary or permanent storage, carriage or transport.

ii. Joint Liability of Operators

When the damage is attributable to more than an operator and cannot be reasonably separated, then all the operators are jointly and severally liable for the damage and the liability lies on all of them (Art. II(3a) of the Vienna Convention).

iii. Exoneration of Liability

The operator will be exonerated from liability:

1) If an individual is liable for the damage caused by his act or omission (Art. 6/1 of the Vienna Convention, Art. 2/2 of the Brussels Convention in the Field of Maritime Carriage of Nuclear Material).

2) If the damage caused directly by nuclear incident due to an act of armed conflict, hostilities, civil war, insurrection or except insofar as the legislation of the Contracting Party in whose territory the nuclear installation is situated may provide to the contrary, a grave natural disaster of an exceptional character (Art. 9 of the Paris Convention).[2]

It appears from the five Conventions mentioned in P. 72, that the liability for nuclear damage falls on the operator of the nuclear installation because he is responsible for its operation, unless he proves that the liability falls on a third party, the operator must have evidence on the liability of the third party. Anyhow the circumstances of the incident can indicate on whom the liability falls upon.

The damage is not enough for considering the liability of the operator but the victim should prove the operator's liability by not taking precautions or measures necessary to prevent the incident or there was a fault the operator is responsible for.

---

[1] - A 'Nuclear Incident' means any occurance or succession of occurances having the same origin which causes damage, provided that such occurance or succession of occurances, or any of the damage caused, arises out of the results from the radioactive properties, or a combination of radioactive properties with toxic, explosive, or other hazardous properties of nuclear fuel or radioactive prodicts or waste or with any of them (Art. 1 of the Paris Convention).

[2] - Although the exoneration of the operator from liability according to Article 9 of the Paris Convention in the cases provided in this Article. But it is the accidents of nuclear weapons which cause great fear and alarm. Any incident will create great and terrible danger to the environment, the atmosphere, destruction and fire which extend to more than 100 square miles and power of explosion to about 200 kilotons.

So the necessity of elimination of all nuclear weapons from the Earth and the universal ban on nuclear weapons are urgent for the protection of the global environment and humankind.

Although some recent treaties on partial nuclear disarmament were concluded e.g. SALT II (1979), INF (1987), START 1 (1991) and START 2 (1992). On the other hand latest news reports have been published in the daily newspapers about the nuclear theft of radioactive materials which threaten the international security, and so it is necessary to tighten the control and to prevent the smuggling of nuclear materials and substances from nuclear sites and installations. The Daily Mail on 20 Auugst 1994 said 'Nuclear theft is rife, admit Russians'. The Daily Mail commentator, Mark Almond, warned of the danger of smuggling nuclear materials.

Section 3 - Dumping

Dumping is deliberate disposal of wastes which pollute the environment and create danger to human health, safety and the living resources. Dumping can be carried out on land, in rivers and seas. It is very harmful to the environment, national and international law prohibit dumping.

A - Land Dumping

The deliberate land dumping causes great damage to the environment and, pollutes the land and soil. Dumping of refuse, waste including solid, liquid, semi-solid or contained gaseous materials resulting from commercial, mining and agricultural operations and from community activities contaminates the land and causes environmental damage and health risks.[1]
Besides, the chemical and radioactive wastes cause reaction and radiation whose risks extend to the neighbouring areas, regions and may cause rivers, estuaries, beaches, territorial waters or transboundary pollution.

B - Sea Dumping

Sea Dumping is any deliberate disposal at sea of wastes or other matters from vessels, aircraft, platforms or other man-made structures at sea, or any deliberate disposal of vessels, aircraft, or other man-made structures at sea. This is the definition of the Convention on the Prevention of Marine Pollution by Dumping of Wastes and other Matter, signed in London, Mexico City and Washington on 29 December 1972.[2]
Moreover, according to this Convention, the sea dumping does not include:
1) the disposal at sea of wastes or other matter incidental to or derived from normal operation of vessels, aircraft, platforms or other man-made structures at sea, operating for the purpose of disposal of such matter or derived from treatment of such wastes or other matter on such vessels, aircraft, platforms or structures;
2) placement of matter for a purpose other than the mere disposal thereof provided that such placement is not contrary to the aims of this Convention. It is difficult to know the legality of the dumping from the two Paras. of the definition under this Convention, but it seems, prima facie, that the difference between the legal and illegal dumping depends on functional exercise of dumping, if the ship or vessel, aircraft or marine means dumps at sea as an functional treatment of wastes, then the dumping would not be illegal and not violate the Convention.
Also according to Para. C of the Art. III the Convention does not cover the disposal of wastes or other matter directly arising from, or related to the exploration, exploitation and associated off-shore processing of sea-bed mineral resources which will not be covered by the provisions of this Convention.
1. Control of Dumping
Art. 4 of the Convention binds the Parties to prohibit dumping of any wastes or other matter, in whatever form or condition.
But this Article, on the other hand, classifies the wastes into 3 categories for the purpose of dumping:

---

[1] - **Introduction to Global Environment Issues.** Kevin Pickering and Lewis Owen. Routledge 1994. p. 269.
[2] - Kiss (UNEP). Ibid. p. 283.

The Threat Against the Environment

a. Wastes and Matters Prohibited from Dumping
The dumping of wastes or other matter listed in Annex 1 is prohibited.
b. Dumping by Special Permit
Dumping of wastes or other matter in Annex II requires a prior special permit.
c. Dumping by General Permit
The dumping of all other wastes or matter requires a prior general permit.

2. Measures for Ships and Aircraft
The Convention binds the Parties according to Art.VII to take measures concerning the ships and aircraft for the implementation of the Convention:

i All ships and aircraft are registered in the Party's territory regarding dumping.
ii Ships and aircraft loading in its territory or territorial seas matter which is to be dumped.
iii Vessels and aircraft and fixed or floating platforms under its jurisdiction believed to be engaged in dumping.

While Para. 2 of the same Article binds the Parties to take the appropriate measures to prevent and punish any conduct in contravention of the Convention.

It is noted also that Art.2(3b) of the International Convention for the Prevention of Pollution by ships, signed in London on 3 November 1973, provides that discharge of harmful substances from ships which involves any escape, disposal, spilling, leaking, pumping, emitting or emptying does not include dumping in the meaning of the Convention on the Prevention of Marine Pollution by Dumping of Wastes and Other Matter of London of 13 November 1972.

C - International Conventions on Dumping

The general principles of dumping are governed by Arts. 210 and 216 of the Convention on the Law of the Sea. There are three main international Conventions on dumping, e.g. the Convention for the Prevention of Marine Pollution by Dumping from Ships and Aircraft signed in Oslo on 15 February 1972; the Convention on the Prevention of Pollution by Dumping of Wastes and Other Matter, signed in London, Mexico City and Washington on 29 December 1972 and the Protocol for the Prevention of Pollution of the Mediterranean Sea by Dumping from Ships and Aircraft signed in Barcelona on 16 February 1976.

Moreover there are some international conventions which prohibit dumping as one of the causes which pollute the environment.[1]

1. Focus on the Convention on the Law of the Sea
The general principles of the prohibition of harmful dumping are provided by Arts. 210 and 216 of the Convention on the Law of the Sea. These two Articles put the responsibility of prevention

---

[1] - The Conventions cited are:
- Convention on the Protection of the Marine Environment in the Baltic Sea, signed in Helsinki on 22 March 1972, (Arts.2(3a) and 9 on dumping).
- The Convention for the Protection of the Mediterranean Sea against Pollution, signed in Barcelona on 16 February 1976 (Art. 5).
- Kuwait Regional Convention for Cooperation on the Protection of Marine Environment against Pollution, signed in Kuwait on 24 April 1978, (Art. 5).
- Regional Convention for the Conservation at the Red Sea and the Gulf of Aden, of Environment, signed in Jiddah on 14 February 1982 (Art. V binds the parties to prevent dumping from ships and aircraft).
- Protocol for the Protection of the South-East Pacific against Radioactive Contamination, signed in Raipa on 21 September 1989. (Art II prohibits dumping or burial of Radioactive Wastes in the sea, the sea bed or the subsoil thereof).

International Conventions on Dumping

of dumping on the States and international organizations which have jurisdiction of establishing international and global rules for the control and prevention of dumping.

Art. 210 in particular grants powers to the States and competent international organizations to make rules, laws and regulations in order to prevent, reduce and control pollution of the marine environment by dumping.

Moreover, the same Article recognizes the jurisdiction of the State in deciding to grant permits for dumping in territorial waters and exclusive economic zone. Also this Article supports the legality of the role of the State in making binding laws and regulations for the control of dumping in its own jurisdiction.

On the other hand, Art.216 provides for the enforcement of the international rules, standards and the States laws and regulations for the prevention of dumping and the protection of marine environment. The powers of enforcement are granted to:

i to the coastal State,
ii to the flag State,
iii to any State with regard to acts of loading of wastes or other matter within its territory or at its off-shore terminals.

Para.2 of this Article gives legal effect to the proceedings of the State and when they have been commenced other States should respect without the institution of new proceedings.

2. The Ban of Dumping and the States

Although all the Conventions on Dumping ban the dumping of harmful wastes at sea, the most hazardous is nuclear waste which is very dangerous to marine environment and the living resources. But still radioactive wastes are being dumped at sea. Some States accepted the voluntary ban on dumping nuclear wastes, but it is necessary to adopt a mandatory international resolution for banning dumping of radioactive wastes at sea because commentators said radioactive substances in the sea respect no territorial boundaries.[1]

---

[1] - The Times on 13 November 1993.

Chapter 4
ENVIRONMENTAL LEGAL RESPONSIBILITY AND DISPUTES

Environmental responsibility has become one of the great important issues today.
The threats and dangers which are created by the actions of States, their agencies, institutions and public bodies on the one hand and the individuals, legal bodies, private firms, corporations and establishments on the other hand cause damage to the environment. This damage may be very great to the environment locally and globally and may affect other States, individuals and private legal bodies and so disputes arise from the damage caused to the victims.
So in this Chapter the study involves:
Section 1   - The Emergence of Legal Responsibility
Section 2   - Regulation of Disputes
Section 3   - Compensation

Section 1 - The Emergence of Legal Responsibility

The principle of the legal liability for damage caused to the environment and that no-one can use his territory in a manner which causes damage and injury to others without being responsible for the damage which the Arbitral Tribunal applied to the US/Canada Dispute (1941) was an expression of one of the fundamental customary norms which have been accepted for a long time beofre the Arbitral decision.
Moreover, the principles of environmental liability have become global custom, especially when the ICJ confirmed in its judgment in the Nuclear Tests Cases (Australia and New Zealand v France 1970), the Court confirming the principle adopted in the Barcelona Tracton Case (1970) that the duty owed to the international community, it is the duty of the State to respect towards all other States. It is the international community which has interests in these rights which relate to the protection of the environment.
And the other judgment of the ICJ in (UK v Albania; Corfu Case 1949) in which the Court regarded the elementary considerations of humanity to put obligations on the States not to use their territories to cause damage to other States' rights.[1]
Moreover the principle 22 of the Human Environment Conference Declaration of Stockholm has recognized the liability for the environmental damage caused to the victim and the right to compensation and requested the development of the principle of liability and compensation.
Furthermore the principle of the polluter should pay for the damage caused to the environment and the victim, has become a customary rule.[2]

A. The Legal System of Liability
1. The Convention on the Law of the Sea

The Convention on the Law of the Sea (Art. 235) provided for the legal system of liability. It can be considered as a general system of law concerning all damage to the environment,

---

[1] - ICJR. 1949. Dixon & McCorquodale Ibid. p. 453.
[2] - The EEC has accepted this principle as a legal rule in its law. **Protection of the Environment. Official Publications of the EEC.** Luxembourg.

Regulation of Disputes

although the Convention is regarded a special multilateral treaty governs the law of the sea.
Art. 235 provides:
a. States are responsible for the fulfillment of their international obligations concerning the protection and preservation of the marine environment. They shall be liable in accordance with international law.
b. States shall ensure that recourse is available in accordance with their legal systems for prompt and adequate compensation or other relief in respect of all damage caused by pollution of the marine environment, by natural or juridical persons under their jurisdiction.
c. With the objective of assuring prompt and adequate compensation in respect of all damage caused by pollution of the marine environment States shall cooperate in the implementation of existing international law and the further development of international law relating to responsibility and liability for the assessment of, and compensation for, damage and the settlement of related disputes, as well as, where appropriate, development of criteria and procedures for payment of adequate compensation such as compulsory insurance or compensation funds.

2. Other International Conventions
Of course the Convention on the Law of the Sea does not affect other international Conventions regarding the provisions of responsibility and liability. This is understood from the provision of Art. 237 of the Convention on the Law of the Sea. As specific obligations of the States should be considered in a manner consistent with the general principles and objectives of the Convention on the Law of the Sea (Art. 237(2)).

B. Principles of Liability

1. Liability of States Arising from Enforcement Measures
Art. 232 of the Convention on the Law of the Sea provides for the liability of the States regarding any unlawful measures taken regarding the damage of pollution and dumping under Section 6.[1]

2. The Civil Liability
The general rule is that the polluter is responsible for the damage, or the doer of the damage is liable for it to the victim and must pay compensation. This general rule applies to all environmental damage caused by the fault of the person who caused the damage. There is a condition for the legal action against the defendant that his liability must be proved before the court, for the damage otherwise the case will not succeed.
Regarding the civil liability, the person who is liable is cited in the following Conventions.
a. The operator of the installation is liable for the damage (Art. 1/b) of the C. Relating to Civil Liability in the Field of Maritime Carriage of Nuclear Matter,[2] also the Vienna C. on Civil Liability for Nuclear Damage[3], also Art. 6 of the Council of Europe Convention on Civil Liability from Activities Dangerous to the Environment.
b. The Owner of the ship at the time of the incident shall be liable for the damage (Art. III(1)) of International C. on Civil Liability for Oil Pollution of Brussels (1969).[4]

---

[1] - Art. 232 provides: "States shall be liabable for damage or loss attributable to them arising from measures taken pursuant to Section 6 when such measures were unlawful or exceeded those reasonably required in the light of available information. States shall provide for recourse in their Courts for actions in respect of such damage or loss."
[2] - Kiss (UNEP) Selected Multilateral Treaties. Ibid. p. 253.
[3] - Ibid. p. 179.
[4] - Ibid. p. 235.

c. The doer of the damage is liable to the victim for that damage and to pay compensation (Art. VI of the International C. Relating to Intervention on the High Seas in Cases of Oil Pollution Casualties.[1]

Section 2 - Regulation of Disputes

The general rule of settlement of disputes is that all disputes should be settled peacefully according to the Charter of the UN and other international agreements on the peaceful settlement of disputes, e.g., the Convention of the Hague on the Peaceful Settlement of Internaional Disputes (1907). The Environmental disputes have two characters; the one is relating to the disputes about the application and interpretation of the conventions and agreements on environment and the other is relating to liability and responsibility concerning damage and injury caused from the violation of the environmental conventions and agreements.

A. Methods of Settlement of Disputes

States are under a duty to solve their disputes by peaceful means according to Art. 33 of the Charter of the UN. The methods of peaceful settlement are: negotiation, mediation, conciliation, arbitration and judicial recourse.

Disputes can be settled by the agreement of the parties, or by compulsory proceedings according to the general rules of international law or certain provisions in the conventions and treaties, where they give the ICJ or special courts compulsory jurisdiction to settle the dispute, when a party to a dispute applies for its settlement, that is by bringing an action before the court against the other party or parties.

B. Voluntary Methods of Settlement of Disputes

Any dispute which arises between the parties can be settled by the agreement of the parties.[2] Agreement of the parties to settle the dispute by their choice can involve one of the voluntary methods of the settlement of disputes, which are:
1. Negotiation, 2. Mediation, 3. Conciliation and 4. Arbitration.

1. Negotiation

A negotiated settlement of a dispute is the best peaceful method of ending the dispute, by an agreement which is acceptable to the parties of the dispute.

All international treaties, conventions and instruments concerning the settlement of the disputes provide for the principle of negotiation as the best peaceful method of ending the dispute and achieving an agreement accepted by the parties (Art. 33 of the UN Charter, Art. 281 of the Convention on the Law of the Sea and Art 14 of the CCC).

2. Mediation

Mediation can be carried out through the agreement of the parties on the person whom they choose to settle the dispute, or by the initiative of the mediator to offer his **bons offices** and mediate between the parties, in order to reach a friendly settlement of the dispute (Art. 2 of the Hague Convention 1907, Cairo Protocol (1964) Arts. 20-21).

The role of the mediator is limited by the agreement of the parties and subject to their

---

[1] - Ibid. p. 230.
[2] - Art. 280 of the Convention on the Law of the Sea: (Nothing in this Part shall impair the right of any States Parties to agree at any time to settle a dispute between them relating to the interpretation or application of this Convention by any peaceful means of their own choice).

acceptance.

3. Conciliation

Conciliation is also a peaceful method of the settlement of the dispute by the agreement of the parties on the conciliator or conciliators (Commission), in order to investigate the dispute and to study the points of difference which cause the dispute and to endeavour to solve it by a favourable agreement which ends the dispute (Arts. 22-25 of Cairo Protocol[1], and Art. 14/5 and 6 of the CCC).

4. Arbitration

Arbitration is the most popular method of ending the disputes by the agreement of the parties on the procedure of arbitration and the appointment of an arbitrator or arbitrators (Arbitral tribunal) to settle the dispute.[2]

Arbitration is an old method of peaceful settlement of disputes, but it has been developing and becoming very successful in gaining support from parties to disputes all over the world.

Art. 33 of the UN Charter, the Annex VI on Arbitration to the Convention of the Law of the Sea, Art. 14(2b) of the CCC, Art. 27(3a) of the BDC and Art. II of the Optional Protocol Concerning the Compulsory Settlement of Disputes to the Vienna Convention on Civil Liability for Nuclear Damage (1963)[3] provide for arbitration as a voluntary method of ending disputes.

a. Arbitration Proceedings

The benefits of arbitration are that the parties to the dispute choose the judge and the law applicable to the dispute.[4] These benefits have led to the acceptance of arbitration in States disputes (public international law), commercial international arbitration and the disputes between States and individuals.

There are many international conventions on arbitration[5] which put the general rules of arbitration.

The general rules of arbitration recognize the freedom of the parties to choose the procedure, the constitution of the arbitral tribunal and the applicable law. For these reasons arbitration is more acceptable by the parties in the disputes than the courts of justice, besides, it may be less

---

[1] - Documentation Française. Droit International Public. Le Reglement Pacifique Des Differences Entre Etats. 1980. p. 4. Also Art. 27 of the BDC (1992).

[2] - KASTO, Jalil. Le Controle Judiciaire sur les Sentences Artitrales des Contrats Internationaux. Research Study presented to the University of Strasbourg. 1978.

[3] - Art. II of the Protocol gives choice to the parties to resort to arbitration, if they do not want the comcpulsory jurisdiction of ICJ in the settlement of the dispute.

[4] - Art. 37 of the Hague Convention (1907). J. Rideau. L'Arbitrage International (Public et Commercial). Armand Colin. Paris. 1969. p. 7.

[5] - These conventions and instruments are:
- The General Act of Arbitration (1929)
- The European Convention on the Peaceful Settlement of Disputes (1957).
- UN Convention for the Recognition and Execution of Foreign Arbitral Sentences (1958).
- The Geneva Convention on International Commercial Arbitration (1961).
- The Washington Convention on the Settlement of Investment Disputes between States and Foreign Natonals (1965).
- The Council of Europe Convention on Uniform Law of Arbitration (1966).
- Moscow Convention on Settlement of Disputes concerning Scientific and Technical Cooperation (1972).
- Protocol II on Arbitration to the International Convention for the Prevention of Pollution from Ships of London (1973).
- UN Model Law on Arbitration (1985).

costly and more speedily in rendering the decisions or the awards in arbitral disputes.[1]
Moreover, as arbitration has become an international regime, it has been institutionalized by the international conventions on arbitration and the centres of arbitration which adopted its own rules and procedures as the IBRD Centre, London Centre for International Arbitration and other centres for international commercial arbitration.

The important question in arbitration is the agreement of the parties on arbitration (Compromis) which has its validity and may contain many details about the procedures, the constitution of the tribunal and the applicable law. These are fundamental matters in the arbitration and the parties cannot fail to respect after the 'compromis' has been signed by the parties and therefore it cannot be challenged by seizing the courts of justice unless the arbitration is sought. The Courts of Justice cannot intervene unless the agreement on arbitration is void, inapplicable, inoperable or the arbitral tribunal has violated the lex fori and there are many legal points which need the supervision of the courts of justice.[2]

Of course, although the arbitration may be favoured more than the legal proceedings before the courts of justice there are many legal, technical and complicated matters which may hinder the effectiveness of arbitration, besides, if a party to the arbitration agreement likes to contest the arbitration procedures or the enforcement of the arbitral award.

b. The Applicable Law

The applicable law in the arbitration is very important, because it makes it more favourable to the parties as they choose the law which may be known to them more than the law they do not know or do not understand. For this reason the UN Model Law on Arbitration has favoured the applicable law the parties choose as a benefit of this law which ensures the universality of this law, rather than other international conventions on arbitration.

The parties may agree on specific law which must be applied by the atbitral tribunal, or the lex fori of the seat of the arbitral tribunal, and if there is no provision about the applicable law the arbitral tribunal may apply the law of its seat (lex fori) or the more convenient international convention on arbitration.

Of course the applicable law can determine the way in which the award is based on and the legality of the award. So the agreement of the parties on the applicable law is very decisive in arbitration.

C. The Compulsory Jurisdiction of the Court

The compulsory jurisdiction in the settlement of disputes is determined by any convention, treaty or protocol, where there is clear provision which confers upon the ICJ or a special court compulsory jurisdiction to settle the dispute according to the ICJ Statute or any other procedure of the special court, e.g. the Law of the Sea Tribunal Art. 286 of the C. on the Law of the Sea Tribunal (Annex V to the same Convention).

1. The Compulsory Jurisdiction of the ICJ

Usually, or as a general rule, the ICJ has compulsory jurisdiction to settle any legal dispute of international law character if there is special and clear provision in an international instrument confers upon the Court this jurisdiction or if the Parties (States) to the Statute of the Court have accepted the compulsory jurisdiction of the Court in any disputes arise or special disputes

---

[1] - UN Model Law on Arbitration.
[2] - Ibid.

Compensation

between the States.[1]

The ICJ applies its Statute according to Art. 36 which confers upon the Court compulsory jurisdiction to settle the dispute between the Parties, and in exercising its jurisdiction, it applies Art. 38 of its Statute which provides:

a. international conventions, special or general which provide for rules expressly recognized by the States Parties to the disputes;
b. international custom as evidence of general practice accepted as law;
c. the general principles of law recognized by civilized nations;
d. with reserve to Art. 59, the decisions of courts and the doctrine of the qualified authors of different nations are regarded as auxiliary means for determining the rules of law.[2]

2. The present provision does affect the competence of the Court, if the Parties agree to decide according to the principles of equity 'ex acqou et bono'.

2. Law of the Sea Tribunal

A State Party to the C. on the Law of the Sea is bound by Art. 287 to refer or accept the compulsory jurisdiction of Law of the Sea Tribunal when it had made a statement or declaration in signing, joining or ratifying the Convention which expresses its consent to accept the compulsory jurisdiction of the Tribunal to settle the dispute concerning the Convention. The Statute of the Tribunal according to Annex V to the C. of the Law of the Sea is applied to the dispute.

3. The European Court of Justice

The ECJ has compulsory jurisdiction to settle environmental disputes according to Art. 130r of the Maastrict Treaty. Any action for damage to the environment or environmental pollution can be brought before the Court and it has compulsory jurisdiction to settle the dispute which arises between the Member-States and the individuals and legal persons.

Section 3 - Compensation

Compensation is an important subject in modern international law, when the environmental damage caused by humans causes injuries and sufferings to the victims, besides, the harm to the environment and the living resources. The environmental damage may be very great and affects many people and a wide area of the sea or land, or may cause transboundary effects which affect more than two States or a number of States.

Compensation under the international conventions is varied according to damage caused, the conditions of compensation and the persons responsible for compensation, so in this Section the study will concentrate on:

A. The Basis of Compensation

The basis of compensation is related to the principle of social justice which gives to the victim of damage the right to compensation as the victim suffers from the action of the person who caused the damage, and this should bear the burden of the damage by paying the compensation to the victim.

---

[1] - Art. 287 of the C. of the Law of the Sea, Art. 14(2a) of the CCC, Art. 27(3a) of the BDC, Art. 1 of the Optional Protocol Concerning the Compulsory Settlement of Disputes to the Vienna Convention on Civil Liability of Nuclear Damage,

[2] - This Article provides: The decision of the Court binds only the Parties to the dispute in the case.

But still, despite the acceptance of a number of international Conventions the principle of compensation, there is a vacuum in others, because no provision was mentioned in them about the compensation to the victims of damage.

All that can be found in several conventions is that there is an urge on the States to negotiate and cooperate in deciding the principles of liability and compensation.

On the other hand, there are many other considerations about the just and unjust compensation, in considering how much compensation should be paid to the victim especially, for certain damage, as the loss of life which cannot be valued, but it is necessary to pay the descendants of the victim a just compensation, especially when the deceased was the only supporter of them.

Also the discretionary power of the judge to consider the sum of compensation, although it cannot be subject to legal enforcement, but can determine the quality of just and unjust judge.

Moreover, the jurisdiction of the court and the principle of compensation were left in a number of environmental conventions to national law and courts.

So it is difficult to put definite principles.

B. Conditions of Compensation

Conditions of compensation are provided by several international conventions.

Any action of compensation requires that:

1. Damage is Caused

Compensation requires that damage or loss was caused to the environment or to the victim.

2. The Liability

The liability of the defendant must be proved before the court, the plaintiff must prove the liability of the person in relation to the damage.[1]

3. State Responsibility

According to Art. III of the International Convention Relating to Intervention on the High Seas in Cases of Oil Pollution Casualties, the responsibility of the State about any measures taken which were taken unreasonably and inappropriately and caused the loss or damage.

4. Time Bar

The action must be brought before the court within three years[2] or ten years,[3] otherwise the action of compensation would not succeed.

C. Assessment of the Compensation

Although the assessment of compensation depends on the circumstances of each case and the loss or damage caused to the victim or to the property or the environment, but in cases of nuclear incidents and pollution where the damage would be great, so the compensation takes into account the extent of damage.

Although the court has discretionary power to determine the amount of compensation, but in some international conventions the maximum amount of compensation is limited by the convention.

Art. V of the Vienna Convention on Civil Liability for Nuclear Damage limited the liability of the operator by US$5 million for any one incident in each case, while Art. 7.b of the Convention on Third Party Liability in the Field of Nuclear Engery limits the maximum amount of compensation by 15,000,000 European Agreement Units for nuclear incident.

---

[1] - Art. II of the Vienna Convention on Civil Liability for Nuclear Damage.
[2] - Art. VIII of the International Convention on Civil Liability for Oil Pollution Damage.
[3] - Art. VI of the Vienna Convention on Civil Liability for Nuclear Damage.

Compensation

The Brussels Convention Supplementary to the Paris Convention has increased the amount of compensation up to 120 million units of account per incident, Art. 3(a).

Of course, when the convention, treaty or protocol does not provide for the maximum amount of compensation, it is the power of the Court to decide the amount of compensation regarding the damage, which itself determines the suffering, loss, destruction or harm to the victim or the property.

The Court or the judge has to consider all the circumstances which affect the amount of compensation and although it, or he, has absolute discretionary power to determine the amount of compensation but the requirements of justice impose on the court or judge to observe the principles of fairness, reasonablness and social balance between the interests of the parties to the disputes in the case.

CONCLUSION

Modern International Law of the Environment is a magnificent attempt to present the most important issues and problems of the global environment in a concentrated study that gives the reader a sufficient understanding of the most necessary knowledge of the environment, its problems and the law which governs. It is not enough that one should have knowledge about the environment, but must act and contribute to the protection of the environment, care and cooperate locally, nationally, and internationally for the protection of the environment and its improvement for the benefit of the community nationally and internationally.

To know the law of the environment is very necessary because the law is a guarantee of the freedoms and rights you enjoy and ask the others and the State to respect them nationally on the one hand.

And on the other hand, it is international law which recognizes for your State the rights and obligations and its role in the international community. The role of the State has become very necessary, essential and important for the enhancement and protection of the environment.

In concluding the study, the book has presented in the first first Chapter; the emergence of the concept of the environment, the early human understanding of it, and how he protected himself against the environmnetal dangers and threats, the role of religions and how they teach the humans to care for the environment. The formation of the earliest norms of the environment was very essential in order that the earliest society had to respect the necessary rules that save and protect their environment from conflicts and harm.

The great development of the interest in the environment has increased the human understanding of the Earth as a global problem and the need for the development of international law.

Then the second Chapter exposes the problem of the protection of the environment, the role of the State, in making laws, with special emphasis on UK laws on several topics of the environmental issues, e.g. water, conservation, protection of wildlife and nature, clean air, noise, waste, disposal of waste, recycling and planning regarding the human environment, the protection of the work environment (issues) concerning the the civil liability for the damage caused to the environment, there is a special study of the Council of Europe Convention on Civil Liability for Damage Resulting from Activities Dangerous to the Environment, the role of the Maastrict Treaty in improving European Community environment and the living conditions and social environment of workers.

There is also good study of the work environment and the proptection of workers, food, and food hygiene.

The role of the individuals is very important in the protection of the environment as well as they are the ones who get benefits from the improvement of the environment, besides the role of the industrial enterprises, corporations, firms and food chains in the protection of environment and improving the quality of life keeping the greens and combating pollution.

Then the role of international community, the international organizations and the universal action, not only is very important but by working together they ensure the international cooperation in the protection of the environment and increase the universal consciousness and care for it.

The contribution of the UN and its system in the development of international law and cooperation is very magnificent and has been dealt with sufficiently in this chapter.

In Chapter 3, the book deals with the threat against the environment, the pollution, nuclear tests, explosions and contamination and dumping were very well exposed in the light of the relative international conventions.

Conclusion

This chapter is a great effort in presenting very fresh study on a number of international conventions that focused on very concentrated principles of the conventions and their affectiveness in ensuring international cooperation in the protection of the environment.

Chapter 4 has dealt with environmental legal responsibility and disputes. The study concentrated on the emergence of legal responsibility, the legal system of liability, the regulation of disputes, voluntary methods of settlement and the compulsory jurisdiction of the courts and the compensation for loss and damage in environmental disputes.

These are vivid subjects in Modern International Law of the Environment which is a great contribution to the development of this law, its understanding in order to achieve the necessary cooperation of individuals, States and peoples everywhere.

The environment and its law belongs to all without discrimination, everyone has the right to live in a good environment, to enjoy a good life and to be protected by good laws which protect him/her and the environment.

Finally, the book has concentrated great attention to the principles of the Rio Summit and Agenda 21 which called upon all States, peoples and the universal community to work together, cooperate and be kind to Mother Earth, which belongs to everyone, every people and to all humankind. This Book is for.

THE END

MODERN INTERNATIONAL LAW OF THE ENVIRONMENT

NEW ENVIRONMENTAL GLOSSARY

NEW ENVIRONMENTAL GLOSSARY

Agenda 21
Is a global programme of action which has been studied and its plan was proposed by UNCED and presented to the GA to take measures with a view to cooperation of the Member-States of UN and the adoption of the plan in Rio Summit in June 1992.
The Rio Summit has finally adopted Agenda 21 as the future global plan for the environment and development for the coming Century 21.
Agenda 21 is great global strategy for the protection of the environment and sustainable development of our planet.
So it is a great achievement by realizing international cooperation which is based on the collective national policies and international actions for the implementation of this global strategy, Agenda 21, which needs the cooperation of all peoples and their Governments to achieve the results.
So Agenda 21 is quite reasonable legal instrument and collective efforts and policies for the protection of Mother Earth and the economic development of all humankind.
It is great achievement of the Rio Summit.

Anthropogeny
Anthropegeny has different meanings. It is:
i. the origin of man;
ii. the science of humans or humankind in the broadest sense;
iii. the science of the nature of man;
iv. the study of man as an animal;
v. the evolution and changes of the human species by the interaction of ecology and habitat.

Climate Change
Climate change is the change of climate by human directly or indirectly, relating to his/her activities that alter the composition of the global atmosphere in addition to natural climate whose changeable conditions are absorbed over comparable periods of time.

Climate system
Is the totality of the atmosphere includes the atmosphere, hydrosphere, biosphere and geosphere and their interactions.

Dangerous Substance
Is any substances or preparations which have properties that constitute a significant risk for human, the environment or property. It involves any substances or preparations which are explosive, oxidizing, extremely inflammable, flammable, toxic, very toxic, harmful, corrosive, irritant, sensitizing, carcinogenic, mutagenic, toxic for reproduction or dangerous for the environment.

Ecology
The interaction between organisms and their environment that is the relations of humans, animals and plants with their environment.

Ecosystem
Is the dymanic complex of plant, animal and micro-organism communities and their non-living environment interacting as a functional unit.

Emission
Is the release of greenhouse gases or their precursors into the atmosphere over specified areas and periods of time.

Environment
Environment is a broad term, the definition cannot be abstract or total, and so it can be intended to mean a limited area of surroundings. In the broad sense, it can mean local, regional, international or global environment which involves the natural resources, (land, mountains, valleys and plains), water (rivers, seas and oceans), air (clouds and atmosphere), human population, living resources (the fauna and flora) and the physical conditions which affect it, that are

the ecosystems and ecology.

Also environment may mean the moral, social and sanitary conditions of human society which are distinct from the material conditions (economic and natural) of the physical environment.

Under international law, environment is considered a distinct subject which involves the Mother Earth (Global Environment), international community, states, peoples, atmospheric, geographical, economic and natural forces, ecology, ecosystems and development and so the law of the environment governs all these fields internally and internationally; the relations of states and international organizations.

Fauna

The animals of a particular region or period of time.

Michael Allaby - A Dictionary of the Environment:

Flora

i. the plants of a particular region or period of time.
ii. a descriptive list of plant species of such a time or place, often with a key to their identification.

Greenhouse Gases

Are gaseous constituents of the atmosphere, material and anthropogenic that absorb and re-emit infrared radiation.

Green Movements

Green Movements all over the World have great support groups nowadays.

Many groups of different names and nationalities are concentrating great efforts for bringing about popular consciousness for environmental issues at global level.

Some of the green movements are Friends of the Earth and Green Parties in many countries are organizing compaigns on world-wide strategy for care of the environment and the protection of the living resources and calling upon all peoples of the Mother Earth to cooperate effectively with the green movements in achieving good results of their purposes for the improvement and care for the global environment.

There is no doubt that Green Movements have exercised strong pressure on governments in many countries to implement the green strategy, and so many governments have now great local groups and authorities which are fulfilling the green strategies for the benefit of the environment.

Habitat

Any area in the range of migratory species which contains suitable living conditions for that species.

(Convention on the Conservation of Migratory Species of Wild Animals. Bonn) 23.6.1979.

High Seas

mean all parts of the Seas which do not include the territorial sea or the internal waters of the state. High seas are open to all members of the international community, are free from any domination of State ownershp. Are free for navigation, for fishing, to lay submarine cables and pipelines and for flight over (four freedoms of the high seas) according to customary international law.

International Law of the Environment

International Law of the Environment is the rules of law which govern all international environmental relations. International law of the environment is newly classified rules of law which developed in the practice of the States since the appearance of States consciousness and awareness in environmental relations. But this law has been developing significantly after the creation of former League of Nations and afterwards the UN and its specified organizations as UNEP, UNCED and other UN Family Agencies.

International law of the environment involves all international conventions, Protocols and treaties as binding conventional instruments on their parties. Besides, the environmental customary law, which has the force of international custom.

To classify the force of any environmental instruments depends on their source, the method of their adoption and those who accept them whether large, small or few number of States, bilateral, multilateral, organizational instruments or have international support by the international community.

On the other hand, there are many declarations, resolutions, decisions and statements adopted by the international organizations on the environmental issues, the force of these instruments depends on the provisions of any constitution of the organization relevant to the instrument, the method of its adoption, and the qualification of the binding instrument as provided, and thus its force depends on the qualification of a binding resolution or instrument.

But it is necessary to mention that international environmental law includes nowadays many rules of jus cogens as it involves very important and vital issues which concern the global environment and the protection of human communities, health and public safety living resources. They are issues which concern the common interest of humankind or the protection of the Mother Earth.

Management of Hazardous Wastes

Hazardous wastes threaten the environment and human health and safety. For this reason the States, international organizations and individuals are very concerned about the hazardous wastes and their management.

The UNCED has put international strategy for environmentally sound management of hazardous wastes. This strategy involves four priority areas:

1. to prevent and minimize hazardous waste as part of broader approach to change industrial processes and consumers patterns, such as through pollution prevention and clean production technologies. Processing wastes into useful recycled material should feature prominently in this strategy.

2. the second priority is to promote and strengthen institutional capacity in hazardous waste management, and **improve knowledge about health and environmental impacts of hazardous waste.**

3. Is to promote and strengthen international cooperation in the **management of transboundary movements of hazardous waste.**

4. Is to set up an international strategy for the environmentally sound management of hazardous wastes. This implies, inter alia, **the national capacities (States) to detect and halt any illegal attempt to introduce hazardous wastes into any country should be strengthened, besides national laws and international legal instruments (Conventions, protocols and treaties and binding resolutions of international organizations).**

Marine Living Resources

There are thousands of life forms in rivers, seas and oceans, about 20,000 species of fresh-water and salt-water living resources which have been identified, while many more species remain to be discovered.

There are roughly 9,000 species which are harvested. The commercial harvest of fishes, crustaceans and mollusca in 1990 amounted to 98 million metric tons, which is equivalent to the estimated sustainable annual yield from conventional fisheries. Over 80 per cent of the commercial harvest of marine

catch, mainly from coastal and shelf seas within the exclusive economic zones (EEZs) as outlined in the Law of the Sea Convention.
The high seas fisheries represent only 5 per cent of the total world landings.
UNCED Guide to Agendda 21, p78.
It is noted that the Convention on the Law of the Sea (1982) (Art. 1(e)) confers on States the freedom of fishing, while Art. 56(1a) recognizes for the coastal State the sovereign rights over the exclusive economic zone which include exploiting, exploring, conserving and managing the living natural resources.

Nuclear Fuel
Is any material capable of producing energy by a self-sustaining chain process of nuclear fission.

Nuclear Incident
Is any occurrence or series of occurrences having the same origin which causes nuclear damage.

Nuclear Material
Is any nuclear fuel other than natural uranium and depleted uranium, capable of producing energy by self-sustaining chain process of nuclear fission outside a nuclear reactor, either alone or in combination with some other material, and radioactive product of waste.

Organic Food
Food which is produced by using natural fertilizers (animals and plants) without the use of agro-chemicals which damage the environment and the wildlife.
Sainsbury's Pamphlet on the Environment.

People Participation and Responsibility in Environmental Issues
Modern international law of the environment stresses the importance of the role of people in participation of the protection of the environment and the management of its development.
This role is not exercised by men only, but also by women and young people. The UNCED has called upon the most indigenous people and their communities, for participation because, they have special relationship with the environment in which they live. And so, they should be empowered to participate in formulating and implementing laws and policies on resources management and development.
They should be finally involved in consultation, collaboration and cooperation. So they properly have rights and obligations in the protection and management of the environment.
Agenda 21 regards local, national and international communities have great responsibilities. Besides, all organizations, (governmental and non-governmental) share the same responsibility.
Also the role of public bodies, trade unions, businesses and economic institutions are called upon to participate in the protection of environment and to bear the environmental responsibility.
Environmental responsibility is a global necessity.

Pollution
Pollution of the environment means release or escape of waste (into and environmental medium) from:
(a) the land on which controlled waste is treated,
(b) the land on which controlled waste is kept,
(c) the land in or on which controlled waste is deposited,
(d) fixed plant by means of which controlled waste is treated, kept or disposed of,

of substances or articles constituting or resulting from the waste and capable (by reason of the quantity or concentrations involved) of causing harm to man or any other living organisms supported by the environment.
EPA (1990).

Pollution of the Sea
is the introduction by human, directly or indirectly of substances or energy into the marine environment (including estuaries) resulting in such deleterious effects as hazards to human health, harm to living resources and to marine ecosystems, damage to amenities or interference with other legitimate uses of the Sea (Convention on the Prevention of Marine Pollution from Land Based Sources of Paris, 4 June 1974).

Preventive Measures
means any reasonable measures taken by any person in relation to a particular incident to prevent or minimize pollution damage with the exception of well controlled measures and measures taken to protect, repair or replace an installation (Convention on Civil Liability for Oil Pollution and Damage Resulting from Exploration and Exploitation of Seabed Marine Resources of London on May 7 1977).

Radiation
means:
1. energy particles emitted by radioactive materials or any decay into more stable elements.
2. the energy waves found in the eletromagnetic spectrum (a system for classifying energy sent out - 'radiated - from various sources). These include radio waves, micro waves, visible light, x rays and gamma rays.
3. Ordinary meaning is the process of emitting energy waves found in electromagnetic spectrum.
Stuart Elsworth. A Dictionary of the Environment. Paladin. 1990. p. 375.

Technology
Is the accumulation of knowledge and classifying it in sophisticated methods which enable using it efficiently, quickly, for different purposes of life, especially in industry, development, inventions, computer processing and environment.
The Greeks meant by technology the art of producing and using tools.
The international law of the environment and environmental sciences use technology as essential and fundamental companion to their evolution and advance.
According to Art. 5(5) of the Annex II to the Law of the Sea Convention (1982) technology is defined as equipment and know-how which are used for exploration and exploitation of the Resources of the Sea. But technology in general terms involves **pure knowledge and technical know-how which develops industry and invention and is very useful for environmental purposes.**

Transfer of Technology
The Code of Conduct on the Transfer of Technology adopted by (UNCTAD) defined the transfer of technology as "**the transfer of systematic knowledge, for the manufacture of a product, for the application of a process or for rendering of a service and does not extend to the transactions involving the sale or mere lease of goods.**"
Although this definition excludes the sale of goods which may involve high technology and sophisticated computers which are useful for environmental purposes, so transfer of technology is very essential for use in the protection and enhancement of the environment, especially for the developing countries.
Also technology involves biotechnology

which is relevant to the environment. And more important is the **Environmentally sound technology** which the UNCED defined as the total systems of know-how, its classification, procedures, goods, services, equipment, administration of human resources, local capacity and resources and aspects of technology choices.

World Conservation Strategy (WCS)
Is coordinated plans based on cooperation and collaboration of international organizations and the States for the maintenance of the World ecosystems. The strategy aims at the preservation of biodiversity species and their productivity so that they do not become extinct.
Prince Philip (Duke of Edinburgh) in his book, **Down to Earth, Man and the Environment.** p. 41. has put the priority requirements as follows:
a. reservation of prime quality cropland for crops
b. adoption of management practices to maintain the productivity of cropland, grazing land and forests
c. prevention of soil degradation, and restoration of land where soils are already degraded
d. protection of watersheds, especially upper catchment areas
e. maintenance of the support systems of fisheries
f. control of pollution
g. prevention of species extinctions
h. preservation of as many varieties as possible of domesticated and other economic or useful plants, animals and micro-organisms and their wild relatives
i. establishment of a comprehensive network of protected areas, securing the habitats of threatened, unique and other important species, unique ecosystems, and representative samples of ecosystem types

j. regulation of living resource utilisation so that it is sustainable
k. reduction of incidental take
l. maintenance of the habitats of utilised species
m. careful allocation and management of timber concessions.

WTO
World Trade Organization succeeds GATT by 1 January 1995, it reflects the greening of GATT.
That is the Signatory Parties have paid more attention to the environment and its impact on trade relations and international trade law. WTO is a significant achievement of the new international trade law and its link with the environment.
124 States have accepted the change on GATT purposes and principles in order to be WTO in which the environment became an essential issue.

BIBLIOGRAPHY

Adams(W.M.) Green Development. Routledge. 1992
Agora. Trade and Environment. AJIL. Vol. 80. 1992
Aristotle. Politics. Translation by Rackman (H.) William Heisman & Harvard Univeristy Press. 1967
Ball (Simon) and Bell (Stuart). Environmental Law. Blackstone Press. 1991
BIBLE
David Psalm
Issaiah
Jeramiah
John
Liviticus
Paul. Corinthians, Titus
Peter 2
Butti (Luciano). Emissioni Inquinante in Atmosfera. Revista Guiridica dell'Ambiente. No. 5 Anno VIII. 1993.
Carwardine (Mark). The WWF Environment. Optima. 1990.
Christian Science Sentinnel. Responsibility for the Environment. A Spiritual Watch Vol. 94. No. 16. 20.4.1992.
Daily Mail. Nuclear Theft is Rife, Admit Russians. 20 August 1994.
Dix (H.M.) Environmental Pollution. John Wily & Sons. 1981.
Dixion (Martin) & McCorquodale. Cases and Materials on International Law. Blackstone Press. 1991.
Documentation Française. Le Reglement Pacifique Des Differences Entre Etats. Droit International Public. Paris. 1980.
DoE. Environment Protection in Europe
DoE. Environmental Policies of the EEC. 1992
DoE. Global Climate Change. 2nd Edition.
DoE. Green Rights and Responsibilities
DoE. Leaflet on Litter and the Law
DoE. Waste Management and Recycling
DoE. What Can You do For the Environment?
Eisemann (Pierre) et Coustere (Vincent). Petit Manuel de la Jurisprudence de la Cour Internationale de Justice. 2eme Editione. Peadone. Paris. 1971.
Eldridge (Jen) Save Our Planet. Magnet Books. 1987.
Elsworth (Stuart). A Dictionary of the Environment.
Goudie (Andrew). The Human Impact on the Natural Environment. Blackwell. 4th Edition.
Halisbury's Statutes. Butterworths.
Harrisson (Paul). The Third Revolution. Taurus & Co. Ltd & Worldwide for Nature 1992.
Hawkes (Nigel). Nclear Safety. Franklin Wats. 1986.
Hounslow Borough Council. Hounslow Environmental Charter 1992.
Hounslow Borough Council. Hounslow Recycling Guide. 1993.
Information Bureau, British Steel. Recylobedia. 1993.
Information Bureau, British Steel. Steel Can Recycling. 1993.

Bibliography

International Labour Organization. Safety and Health in Construction. Geneva. 1992.
Johnson (Colin). Green Dictionary. Optima Books. 1991.
Kasto (Jalil). Le Contrôle Judiciaire Des Sentences Arbitrales Des Contrats Internationaux. Research Study presented to the University of Strasbourg. 1978.
Kiss (Alexandre). Droit International de l'Environnement. Documentation Française. 1992.
Kiss (Alexandre). La Protection International de l'Environnement. Documentation Française. 1977.
Kiss (Alexandre). Selected Multilateral Treaties in the Field of the Environment. Series 3. United Nations Environment Programme. Nairobi. 1983.
Koran (Cow - Albakara Surat).
Maclachen (Graham). Green Alamanc. Docher Publishers Ltd. 1991.
Mahraj (Huzar) & Singh (Sawan). Philosophy of the Masters. Radha Soami Satsang Beas. 1973.
McCormack. The Global Environmental Movement. Belhaven Press. 1992.
Mellanby (Kenneth). The Biology of Pollution. 2nd Edition. Edward Arnold. 1980.
Mihner (Henry). Sweden Social Democracy in Practice. Oxford University Press. 1990.
Ministry of Agriculture and Food, Safety Department. Food Protection. 1992.
Miss London (Review).
National Westminster Bank. Environment Review. 1993.
Office for the Official Publications of the European Communities. Environment Policy in the European Community. 1992.
Pickering (Kevin) & Owen (Lewis). Introduction to Global Environmental Issues. Routledge. 1994.
Prince Philip (Duke of Edinburgh). Down to Earth, Man and the Environment. Collins. 1988.
Sainsbury's. Pamphlet on the Environment.
Sayth (Struan). The Times Guide to the Environment. 1990.
Surrey County Council. Surrey Caring for our Environment. 3/93.
Schneider (Herman & Leo). Dictionary of Science for Everyone. Paragon Books. 1992.
Tesco. Green Choice, Global Warming and Ozone Depletion.
UNCED. The Global Partnership for Environment and Development. A Guide to Agenda 21. Geneva 1992.
UNCITRAL. UN Model Law on Arbitration. 1985.
UNEP. Environmental Law. Guidelines and Principles. Stockholm Declaration.
UNEP. Register of International Treaties and Other Agreements in the Field of the Environment. Nairobi. 1991.
Veda (Rig). Collection of Hymns. Translation of O.F. Wedy Deniger O'Flenchery. Penguin Books. 1981.
World Commission on Environment and Development. Our Common Future. Oxford University Press. 1988.
World Commission on Environment and Development. Food 2000. Zed Books. 1987.

ANNEX 1

UNITED NATIONS CONVENTION ON BIOLOGICAL DIVERSITY

5 JUNE 1992

FULL TEXT

Preamble

The Contracting Parties,

<u>Conscious</u> of the intrinsic value of biological diversity and of the ecological, genetic, social, economic, scientific, educational, cultural, recreational and aesthetic values of biological diversity and its components,
<u>Conscious also</u> of the importance of biological diversity for evolution and for maintaining life sustaining systems of the biosphere,
<u>Affirming</u> that the conservation of biological diversity is a common concern of humankind,
<u>Reaffirming</u> that States have sovereign rights over their own biological resources,
<u>Reaffirming also</u> that States are responsible for conserving their biological diversity and for using their biological resources in a sustainable manner,
<u>Concerned</u> that biological diversity is being significantly reduced by certain human activities,
<u>Aware</u> of the general lack of information and knowledge regarding biological diversity and of the urgent need to develop scientific, technical and institutional capacities to provide the basic understanding upon which to plan and implement appropriate measures,
<u>Noting</u> that it is vital to anticipate, prevent and attack the causes of significant reduction or loss of biological diversity at source,
<u>Noting also</u> that where there is a threat of significant reduction or loss of biological diversities, lack of full scientific certainty should not be used as a reason for postponing measures to avoid or minimize such a threat,
<u>Noting further</u> that the fundamental requirement for the conservation of biological diversity is the in-situ conservation of ecosystems and natural habitats and the maintenance and recovery of viable population of species in their natural surroundings,
<u>Notify further</u> that <u>ex-situ</u> measures, preferably in the country of origin, also have an important role to play,
<u>Recognizing</u> the close and traditional dependence of many indigenous and local communities embodying traditional lifestyles on biological resources, and the desirability of sharing equitable benefits arising from the use of traditional knowledge, innovation and practices relevant to the conservation of biological diversity and the sustainable use of its components,
<u>Recognizing also</u> the vital role that women play in the conservation and sustainable use of biological diversity and affirming the need for the full participation of women at all levels of policy-making and implementation for biological diversity conservation,
<u>Stressing</u> the importance of, and the need to promote, international, regional and global cooperation among States and intergovernmental organizations and the non-governmental sector

for the conservation of biological diversity and the sustainable use of its components,
Acknowledging that the provision of new and additional financial resources and appropriate access to relevant technologies can be expected to make a substantial difference in the world's ability to address the loss of biological diversity,
Acknowledging further that special provision is required to meet the needs of developing countries, including the provision of new and additional financial resources and appropriate access to relevant technologies,
Noting in this regard the special conditions of the least developed countries and small island States,
Acknowledging that substantial investments are required to conserve biological diversity and that there is the expectation of a broad range of environmental, economic and social benefits from those investments,
Recognizing that economic and social development and poverty eradication are the first and overriding priorities of developing countries,
Aware that conservation and sustainable use of biological diversity is of critical importance for meeting the food, health and other needs of the growing world population, for which purpose access to and sharing of both genetic resources and technologies are essential,
Noting that, ultimately, the conservation and sustainable use of biological diversity will strengthen friendly relations among States and contribute to peace for humankind,
Desiring to enhance and complement existing international arrangements for the conservation of biological diversity and sustainable use of its components, and
Determined to conserve and sustainabley use biological diversity for the benefit of present and future generations,

Have agreed as follows:

ARTICLE 1
OBJECTIVES
The objectives of this Convention, to be pursued in accordance with its relevant provisions, are the conservation of biological diversity, the sustainable use of its components and the fair and equitable sharing of the benefits arising out of the utilization of genetic resources, including by appropriate access to genetic resources and by appropriate transfer of relevant technologies, taking into account all rights over those resources and to technologies, and by appropriate funding.

ARTICLE 2
USE OF TERMS
For the purposes of this Convention:
"Biological diversity" means the variability among living organisms from all sources including, *inter alia*, terrestrial, marine and other aquatic ecosystems and the ecological complexes of which they are part; this includes diversity within species, between species and of ecosystems.
"Biological resources" includes genetic resources, organisms or parts thereof, populations, or any other biotic component of ecosystems with actual or potential use or value for humanity.
"Biotechnology" means any technological application that uses biological systems, living organisms, or derivations thereof, to make or modify products or processes for specific use.

"Country of origin of genetic resources" means the country which possesses those genetic resources in *in-situ* conditions.

"Country providing genetic resources" means the country supplying genetic resources collected from *in-situ* sources, including populations of both wild and domesticated species, or taken from *ex-situ* sources, which may or may not have originated in that country.

"Domesticated or cultivated species" means species in which the evolutionary process has been influenced by humans to meet their needs.

"Ecosystems" means a dynamic complex of plant, animal and micro-organism communities and their non-living environment interacting as a functional unit.

"Ex-situ conservation" means the conservation of components of biological diversity outside their natural habitats.

"Genetic material" means any material of plant, animal, microbial or other origin containing functional units of heredity.

"Genetic resources" means genetic material or actual or potential value.

"Habitat" means the place or type of site where an organism or population naturally occurs.

"In-situu conditions" means conditions where genetic resources exist within ecosystems and natural habitats, and, in the case of domesticated or cultivated species, in the surroundings where they have developed their distinctive properties.

"In-situ conservation" means the conservation of ecosystems and natural habitats and the maintenance and recovery of viable populations of species in their natural surrounding and, in the case of domesticated or cultivated species, in the surroundings where they have developed their distinctive properties.

"Protected area" means a geographically defined area which is designated or regulated and managed to achieve specific conservation objectives.

"Regional economic integration organization" means an organization constituted by sovereign States of a given region, to which its member States have transferred competence in respect of matters governed by this Convention and which has been duly authorized, in accordance with its internal procedures, to sign, ratify, accept, approve or accede to it.

"Sustainable use" means the use of components of biological diversity in a way and at a rate that does not lead to the long-term decline of biological diversity, thereby maintaining its potential to meet the needs and aspirations of present and future generations.

"Technology" includes biotechnology.

ARTICLE 3
PRINCIPLE

States have, in accordance with the Charter of the United Nations and the principles of international law, the sovereign rights to exploit their own resources pursuant to their own environmental policies, and the responsibility to ensure that activities within their jurisdiction or control do not cause damage to the environment of other States or of areas beyond the limits of national jurisdiction.

ARTICLE 4
JURISDICTIONAL SCOPE

Subject to the rights of other States, and except as otherwise expressly provided in this Convention, the provisions of this Convention apply, in relation to each Contracting Party:

(a) In the case of components of biological diversity, in areas within the limits of its national jurisdiction; and
(b) In the case of processes and activities, regardless of where their effects occur, carried out under its jurisdiction or control, within the area of its national jurisdiction or beyond the limits of national jurisdiction.

ARTICLE 5
COOPERATION
Each Contracting Party shall, as far as possible and as appropriate, cooperate with other Contracting Parties, directly or, where appropriate, through component international organizations, in respect of areas beyond national jurisdiction and on other matters of mutual interest, for the conservation and sustainable use of biological diversity.

ARTICLE 6
GENERAL MEASURES FOR CONSERVATION AND SUSTAINABLE USE
Each Contracting Party shall, in accordance with its particular conditions and capabilities:
(a) Develop national strategies, plans or programmes for the conservation and sustainable use of biological diversity or adapt for this purpose existing strategies, plans or programmes which shall reflect, *inter alia,* the measures set out in this Convention relevant to the Contracting Party concerned; and
(b) Integrate, as far as possible and as appropriate, the conservation and sustainable use of biological diversity into relevant sectoral or cross-sectoral plans, programmes and policies.

ARTICLE 7
IDENTIFICATION AND MONITORING
Each Contracting Party shall, as far as possible and as appropriate, in particular for the purposes of Articles 8 - 10:
(a) Identify components of biological diversity important for its conservation and sustainable use having regard to the indicative list of categories set down in Annex I;
(b) Monitor, through sampling and other techniques, the components of biological diversity identified pursuant to subparagraph (a) above, paying particular attention to those requiring urgent conservation measures and those which offer the greatest potential for sustainable use;
(c) Identify processes and categories of activities which have or are likely to have significant adverse impacts on the conservation and sustainable use of biological diversity, and monitor their effects through sampling and other techniques; and
(d) Maintain and organize, by any mechanism data, derived from identification and monitoring activities pursuant to subparagraphs (a), (b) and (c) above.

ARTICLE 8
IN-SITU CONSERVATION
Each Contracting Party shall, as far as possible and as appropriate:
(a) Establish a system of protected areas or areas where special measures need to be taken to conserve biological diversity;
(b) Develop, where necessary, guidelines for the selection, establishment and management of protected areas or areas where special measures need to be taken to conserve biological

diversity;
(c) Regulate or manage biological resources important for the conservation of biological diversity whether within or outside protected areas, with a view to ensuring their conservation and sustainable use;
(d) Promote the protection of ecosystems, natural habitats and the maintenance of viable populations of species in natural surroundings;
(e) Promote environmentally sound and sustainable development in areas adjacent to protected areas with a view to furthering protection of these areas;
(f) Rehabilitate and restore degraded ecosystems and promote the recovery of threatened species, *inter alia*, through the development and implementation of plans or other management strategies;
(g) Establish or maintain means to regulate, manage or control the risks associated with the use and release of living modified organisms resulting from biotechnology which are likely to have adverse environmental impacts that could affect the conservation and sustainable use of biological diversity, taking also into account the risks to human health;
(h) Prevent the introduction of, control or eradicate those alien species which threaten ecosystems, habitats or species;
(i) Endeavour to provide the conditions needed for compatibility between present uses and the conservation of biological diversity and the sustainable use of its components;
(j) Subject to its national legislation, respect, preserve and maintain knowledge, innovations and practices of indigenous and local communities embodying traditional lifestyles relevant for the conservation and sustainable use of biological diversity and promote their wider application with the approval and involvement of the holders of such knowledge, innovations and practices and encourage the equitable sharing of the benefits arising from the utilization of such knowledge, innovations and practices;
(k) Develop or maintain necessary legislation and/or other regulatory provisions for the protection of threatened species and populations;
(l) Where a significant adverse effect on biological diversity has been determined pursuant to Article 7, regulate or manage the relevant processes and categories of activities; and
(m) Cooperate in providing financial and other support for *in-situ* conservation outlined in subparagraphs (a) to (l) above, particularly to developing countries.

ARTICLE 9
EX-SITU CONSERVATION

Each Contracting Party shall, as far as possible and as appropriate, and predominantly for the purposes of complementing *in-situ* measures:
(a) Adopt measures for the *ex-situ* conservation of components of biological diversity, preferably in the country of origin of such components;
(b) Establish and maintain facilities for *ex-situ* conservation of and research on plants, animals and micro-organisms, preferably in the country of origin of genetic resources;
(c) Adopt measures for the recovery and rehabilitation of threatened species and for their reintroduction into their natural habitats under appropriate conditions;
(d) Regulate and manage collection of biological resources from natural habitats for *ex-situ* conservation purposes so as not to threaten ecosystems and *in-situ* populations of species, except where special temporary *ex-situ* measures are required under subparagraph (c) above; and

(e) Cooperate in providing financial and other support for *ex-situ* conservation outlined in subparagraphs (a) and (d) above and in the establishment and maintenance of *ex-situ* conservation facilities in developing countries.

ARTICLE 10
SUSTAINABLE USE OF COMPONENTS OF BIOLOGICAL DIVERSITY

Each Contracting Party shall, as far as possible and as appropriate:
(a) Integrate consideration of the conservation and sustainable use of biological resources into national decision-making;
(b) Adopt measures relating to the use of biological resources to avoid or minimize adverse impacts on biological diversity;
(c) Protect and encourage customary use of biological resources in accordance with traditional cultural practices that are compatible with conservation or sustainable use requirements;
(d) Support local populations to develop and implement remedial action in degraded areas where biological diversity has been reduced; and
(e) Encourage cooperation between its governmental authorities and its private sector in developing methods for sustainable use of biological resources.

ARTICLE 11
INCENTIVE MEASURES

Each Contracting Party shall, as far as possible and as appropriate, adopt economically and socially sound measures that act as incentives for the conservation and sustainable use of components of biological diversity.

ARTICLE 12
RESEARCH AND TRAINING

The Contracting Parties, taking into account the special needs of developing countries, shall;
(a) Establish and maintain programmes for scientific and technical education and training in measures for the identification, conservation and sustainable use of biological diversity and its components and provide support for such education and training for the specific needs of developing countries;
(b) Promote and encourage research which contributes to the conservation and sustainable use of biological diversity, particularly in developing countries, *inter-alia*, in accordance with decisions of the Conference of the Parties taken in consequences of recommendations of the Subsidiary Body on Scientific, Technical and Technological Advice; and
(c) In keeping with the provisions of Articles 16, 18 and 20, promote and cooperate in the use of scientific advances in biological diversity research in developing methods for conservation and sustainable use of biological resources.

ARTICLE 13
PUBLIC EDUCATION AND AWARENESS

The Contracting Parties shall:
(a) Promote and encourage understanding of the importance of, and the measures required for, the conservation of biological diversity, as well as its propagation through media, and the inclusion of these topics in educational programmes; and

(b) Cooperate, as appropriate, with other States and international organizations in developing educational and public awareness programmes, with respect to conservation and sustainable use of biological diversity.

ARTICLE 14
IMPACT ASSESSMENT AND MINIMIZING ADVERSE IMPACTS

1. Each Contracting Party, as far as possible and as appropriate, shall:
(a) Introduce appropriate procedures requiring environmental impact assessment of its proposed projects that are likely to have significant adverse effects on biological diversity with a view to avoiding or minimizing such effects and, where appropriate, allow for public participation in such procedures;
(b) Introduce appropriate arrangements to ensure that the environmental consequences of its programmes and policies that are likely to have significant adverse impacts on biological diversity are duly taken into accounts;
(c) Promote, on the basis of reciprocity, notification, exchange of information and consultation on activities under their jurisdiction or control which are likely to significantly affect adversely the biological diversity of other States or areas beyond the limits of national jurisdiction, by encouraging the conclusion of bilateral, regional or multilateral arrangements, as appropriate;
(d) In the case of imminent or grave danger or damage, originating under its jurisdiction or control, to biological diversity within the area under jurisdiction of other States or in areas beyond the limits of national jurisdiction, notify immediately the potentially affected States of such danger or damage, as well as initiate action to prevent or minimize such danger or damage; and
(e) Promote national arrangements for emergency responses to activities or events, whether caused naturally or otherwise, which present a grave and imminent danger to biological diversity and encourage international cooperation to supplement such national efforts and, where appropriate and agreed by the States or regional economic integration organizations concerned, to establish joint contingency plans.
2. The Conference of the Parties shall examine, on the basis of studies to be carried out, the issue of liability and redress, including restoration and compensation, for damage to biological diversity, except where such liability is a purely internal matter.

ARTICLE 15
ACCESS TO GENETIC RESOURCES

1. Recognizing the sovereign rights of States over their natural resources, the authority to determine access to genetic resources rests with the national governments and is subject to national legislation.
2. Each Contracting Party shall endeavour to create conditions to facilitate access to genetic resources for environmentally sound uses by other Contracting Parties and not to impose restrictions that run counter to the objectives of this Convention.
3. For the purposes of this Convention, the genetic resources being provided by a Contracting Party, as referred to in this Article and Articles 16 and 19, are only those that are provided by Contracting Parties that are countries or origin or such resources or by the Parties that have acquired the genetic resources in accordance with this Convention.
4. Access, where granted, shall be on mutually agreed terms and subject to the provisions of

this Article.

5. Access to genetic resources shall be subject to prior informed consent of the Contracting Party providing such resources, unless otherwise determined by that Party.

6. Each Contracting Party shall endeavour to develop and carry out scientific research based on genetic resources provided by other Contracting Parties with the full participation of, and where possible in, such Contracting Parties.

7. Each Contracting Party shall take legislative, administrative or policy measures, as appropriate, and in accordance with Articles 16 and 19 and, where necessary, through the financial mechanism established by Articles 20 and 21 with the aim of sharing in a fair and equitable way the results of research and development and the benefits arising from the commercial and other utilization of genetic resources with the Contracting Party providing such resources. Such sharing shall be upon mutually agreed terms.

ARTICLE 16
ACCESS TO AND TRANSFER OF TECHNOLOGY

1. Each Contracting Party, recognizing that technology includes biotechnology, and that both access to and transfer of technology among Contracting Parties are essential elements for the attainment of the objectives of this Convention, undertakes subject to the provisions of this Article to provide and/or facilitate access for and transfer to other Contracting Parties of technologies that are relevant to the conservation and sustainable use of biological diversity or make use of genetic resources and do not cause significant damage to the environment.

2. Access to and transfer of technology referred to in paragraph 1 above to developing countries shall be provided and/or facilitated under fair and most favourable terms, including on concessional and preferential terms where mutually agreed, and, where necessary, in accordance with the financial mechanism established by Articles 20 and 21. In the case of technology subject to patents and other intellectual property rights, such access and transfer shall be provided on terms which recognize and are consistent with the adequate and effective protection of intellectual property rights. The application of this paragraph shall be consistent with paragraphs 3, 4 and 5 below.

3. Each Contracting Party shall take legislative, administrative or policy measures, as appropriate, with the aim that Contracting Parties, in particular those that are developing countries, which provide genetic resources, on mutually agreed terms, including technology protected by patents and other intellectual property rights, where necessary, through the provisions of Articles 20 and 21 and in accordance with international law and consistent with paragraphs 4 and 5 below.

4. Each Contracting Party shall take legislative, administrative or policy measures, as appropriate, with the aim that the private sector facilitates access to, joint development and transfer of technology referred to in paragraph 1 above for the benefit of both governmental institutions and the private sector of developing countries and in this regard shall abide by the obligations included in paragraphs 1, 2 and 3 above.

5. The Contracting Parties, recognizing that patents and other intellectual property rights may have an influence on the implementation of this Convention, shall cooperate in this regard subject to national legislative and international law in order to ensure that such rights are supportive of and do not run counter to its objectives.

ARTICLES 17
EXCHANGE OF INFORMATION

1. The Contracting Parties shall facilitate the exchange of information, from all publicly available sources, relevant to the conservation and sustainable use of biological diversity, taking into account the special needs of developing countries.
2. Such exchange of information shall include exchange of results of technical, scientific and socio-economic research, as well as information on training and surveying programmes, specialized knowledge, indigenous and traditional knowledge as such and in combination with the technologies referred to in Article 16, paragraph 1. It shall also, where feasible, include repatriation of information.

ARTICLE 18
TECHNICAL AND SCIENTIFIC COOPERATION

1. The Contracting Parties shall promote international technical and scientific cooperation in the field of conservation and sustainable use of biological diversity, where necessary, through the appropriate international and national institutions.
2. Each Contracting Party shall promote technical and scientific cooperation with other Contracting Parties, in particular developing countries, in implementing this Convention, *inter alia*, through the development and implementation of national policies. In promoting such cooperation, special attention should be given to the development and strengthening of national capabilities, by means of human resources development and institution building.
3. The Conference of the Parties, at its first meeting, shall determine how to establish a clearing-house mechanism to promote and facilitate technical and scientific cooperation.
4. The Contracting Parties shall, in accordance with national legislation and policies, encourage and develop methods of cooperation for the development and use of technologies, including indigenous and traditional technologies, in pursuance of the objectives of this Convention. For this purpose, the Contracting Parties shall also promote cooperation in the training of personnel and exchange of experts.
5. The Contracting Parties shall, subject to mutual agreement, promote the establishment of joint research programmes and joint ventures for the development of technologies relevant to the objectives of this Convention.

ARTICLE 19
HANDLING OF BIOTECHNOLOGY AND DISTRIBUTION OF ITS BENEFITS

1. Each Contracting Party shall take legislative, administrative or policy measures, as appropriate, to provide for the effective participation in biotechnological research activities by those Contracting Parties, especially developing countries, which provide the genetic resources for such research, and where feasible in such Contracting Parties.
2. Each Contracting Party shall take all practicable measures to promote and advance priority access on a fair and equitable basis by Contracting Parties, especially developing countries, to the results and benefits arising from biotechnologies based upon genetic resources provided by those Contracting Parties. Such access shall be on mutually agreed terms.
3. The Parties shall consider the need for and modalities of a protocol setting out appropriate procedures, including, in particular, advance informed agreement, in the field of the safe transfer, handling and use of any living modified organisms resulting from biotechnology that

UN Convention on Biological Diversity

may have adverse effect on the conservation and sustainable use of biological diversity.
4. Each Contracting Party shall, directly or by requiring any natural or legal person under its jurisdiction providing the organisms referred to in paragraph 3 above, provide any available information about the use and safety regulations required by that Contracting Party in handling such organisms, as well as any available information on the potential adverse impact of the specific organisms concerned to the Contracting Party into which those organisms are to be introduced.

ARTICLE 20
FINANCIAL RESOURCES

1. Each Contracting Party undertakes to provide, in accordance with its capabilities, financial support and incentives in respect of those national activities which are intended to achieve the objectives of this Convention, in accordance with its national plans, priorities and programmes.
2. The developed country Parties shall provide new and additional financial resources to enable developing country Parties to meet the agreed full incremental cost to them of implementing measures which fulfill the obligations of this Convention and to benefit from its provisions and which agreed costs are agreed between a developing country Party and the institutional structure referred to in Article 21, in accordance with policy, strategy, programme priorities and eligibility criteria and an indicative list of incremental costs established by the Conference of the Parties. Other Parties, including countries undergoing the process of transition to a market economy, may voluntarily assume the obligations of the developed country Parties. For the purposes of this Article, the Conference of the Parties, shall at its first meeting establish a list of developed county Parties and other Parties which voluntarily assume the obligations of the developed country Parties. The Conference of the Parties shall periodically review and if necessary amend the list. Contributions from other countries and sources on a voluntary basis would also be encouraged. The implementation of these commitments shall take into account the need for adequacy, predictability and timely flow of funds and the importance of burden-sharing among the contributing Parties included in the list.
3. The developed country Parties may also provide, and developing country Parties avail themselves of, financial resources related to the implementation of this Convention through bilateral, regional and other multilateral channels.
4. The extent to which developing country Parties will effectively implement their commitments under this Convention will depend on the effective implementation by developed country Parties on their commitments under this Convention related to financial resources and transfer of technology and will take fully into account the fact that economic and social development and eradication of poverty are the first and overriding priorities of the developing country Parties.
5. The Parties shall take full account of the specific needs and special situation of least developed countries in their actions with regard to funding and transfer of technology.
6. The Contracting Parties shall also take into consideration the special conditions resulting from the dependence on, distribution and location of, biological diversity within developing country Parties, in particular small island States.
7. Consideration shall also be given to the special situation of developing countries, including those that are most environmentally vulnerable, such as those with arid and semi-arid zones, coastal and mountainous areas.

UN Convention on Biological Diversity

ARTICLE 21
FINANCIAL MECHANISMS

1. There shall be a mechanism for the provision of financial resources to developing country Parties for purposes of this Convention on a grant or concession basis the essential elements of which are described in this Article. The mechanism shall function under the authority and guidance of, and be accountable to, the Conference of the Parties for purposes of this Convention. The operations of the mechanism shall be carried out by such institutional structures as may be decided upon by the Conference of the Parties at its first meeting. For purposes of this Convention, the Conference of the Parties shall determine the policy, strategy, programme priorities and eligibility criteria relating to the access to and utilization of such resources. The contributions shall be such as to take into account the need for predictability, adequacy and timely flow of funds referred to in Article 20 in accordance with the amount of resources needed to be decided periodically by the Conference of the Parties and the importance of burden-sharing among the contributing Parties included in the list referred to in Article 20, paragraph 2. Voluntary contributions may also be made by the developed country Parties and by other countries and sources. The mechanism shall operate within a democratic and transparent system of governance.

2. Pursuant to the objectives of this Convention, the Conference of the Parties shall at its first meeting determine the policy, strategy and programme priorities, as well as detailed criteria and guidelines for eligibility for access to and utilization of the financial resources including monitoring and evaluation on a regular basis of such utilization. The Conference of the Parties shall decide on the arrangement to give effect to paragraph 1 above after consultation with the institutional structure entrusted with the operation of the financial mechanisms.

3. The Conference of the Parties shall review the effectiveness of the mechanism established under this Article, including the criteria and guidelines referred to in paragraph 2 above, not less than two years after the entry into force of this Convention and thereafter on a regular basis. Based on such review, it shall take appropriate action to improve the effectiveness of the mechanism if necessary.

4. The Contracting Parties shall consider strengthening existing financial institutions to provide financial resources for the conservation and sustainable use of biological diversity.

ARTICLE 22
RELATIONSHIP WITH OTHER INSTITUTIONAL CONVENTIONS

1. The provisions of this Convention shall not affect the rights and obligations of any Contracting Party deriving from any existing international agreement, except where the exercise of those rights and obligations would cause a serious damage or threat to biological diversity.

2. Contracting Parties shall implement this Convention with respect to the marine environment consistently with the rights and obligations of States under the law of the sea.

ARTICLE 23
CONFERENCE OF THE PARTIES

1. A Conference of the Parties is hereby established. The first meeting of the Conference of the Parties shall be convened by the Executive Director of the United Nations Environment Programme not later than one year after the entry into force of this Convention. Thereafter, ordinary meetings of the Conference of the Parties shall be held at regular intervals to be

determined by the Conference at its first meeting.

2. Extraordinary meetings of the Conference of the Parties shall beheld at such other times as may be deemed necessary by the Conference, or at the written request of any Party, provided that, within six months of the request being communicated to them by the Secretariat, it is supported by at least one third of the Parties.

3. The Conference of the Parties shall by consensus agree upon and adopt rules of procedure for itself and for any subsidiary body it may establish, as well as financial rules governing the funding of the Secretariat. At each ordinary meeting, it shall adopt a budget for the financial period until the next ordinary meeting.

4. The Conference of the Parties shall keep under review the implementation of this Convention, and, for this purpose, shall:

(a) Establish the form and the intervals for transmitting the information to be submitted in accordance with Article 26 and consider such information as well as reports submitted by any subsidiary body;

(b) Review scientific, technical and technological advice on biological diversity provided in accordance with Article 25;

(c) Consider and adopt, as required, proposals in accordance with Article 28;

(d) Consider and adopt, as required, in accordance with Articles 29 and 30, amendments to this Convention and its annexes;

(e) Consider amendments to any protocol, as well as to any annexes thereto, and, if so decided, recommend their adoption to the parties to the protocol concerned;

(f) Consider and adopt, as required, in accordance with Article 30, additional annexes to this Convention;

(g) Establish such subsidiary bodies, particularly to provide scientific and technical advice, as are deemed necessary for the implementation of this Convention;

(h) Contact, through the Secretariat, the executive bodies of conventions dealing with matters covered by this Convention with a view to establishing appropriate forms of cooperation with them; and

(i) Consider and undertake any additional action that may be required for the achievement of the purposes of this Convention in the light of experience gained in its operation.

5. The United Nations, its specialized agencies and the International Atomic Energy Agency, as well as any State not Party to this Convention, may be represented as observers at meetings of the Conference of the Parties. Any other body or agency, whether governmental or non-governmental, qualified in fields relating to conservation and sustainable use of biological diversity, which has informed the Secretariat of its wish to be represented as an observer at a meeting of the Conference of the Parties, may be admitted unless at least one third of the Parties present object. The admission and participation of observers shall be subject to the rules of procedure adopted by the Conference of the Parties.

ARTICLE 24
SECRETARIAT

1. A secretariat is hereby established. Its functions shall be:

(a) To arrange for and service meetings of the Conference of the Parties provided for in Article 23;

(b) To perform the functions assigned to it by any protocol;

(c) To prepare reports on the execution of its functions under this Convention and present them to the Conference of the Parties;
(d) To coordinate with other relevant international bodies and, in particular to enter into such administrative and contractual arrangements as may be required for the effective discharge of its functions; and
(e) To perform such other functions as may be determined by the Conference of the Parties.
2. At its first ordinary meeting, the Conference of the Parties shall designate the secretariat from amongst those existing competent international organizations which have signified their willingness to carry out the secretariat functions under this Convention.

ARTICLE 25
SUBSIDIARY BODY ON SCIENTIFIC, TECHNICAL AND TECHNOLOGICAL ADVICE

1. A subsidiary body for the provision of scientific, technical and technological advice is hereby established to provide the Conference of the Parties and, as appropriate, its other subsidiary bodies with timely advice relating to the implementation of this Convention. This body shall be open to participation by all Parties and shall be multidisciplinary. It shall comprise government representatives competent in the relevant field of expertise. It shall report regularly to the Conference of the Parties on all aspects of its work.
2. Under the authority of and in accordance with guidelines laid down by the Conference of the Parties, and upon its request, this body shall:
(a) Provide scientific and technical assessment of the status of biological diversity;
(b) Prepare scientific and technical assessments of the effects of types of measures taken in accordance with the provisions of this Convention:
(c) Identify innovative, efficient and state-of-the-art technologies and know-how relating to the conservation and sustainable use of biological diversity and advise on the ways and means of promoting developing and/or transferring such technologies;
(d) Provide advice on scientific programmes and international cooperation in research and development related to conservation and sustainable use of biological diversity; and
(e) Respond to scientific, technical, technological and methodological questions that the Conference of the Parties and its subsidiary bodies may put to the body.
3. The functions, terms of reference, organization and operation of this body may be further elaborated by the Conference of the Parties.

ARTICLE 26
REPORTS

Each Contracting Party shall, at intervals to be determined by the Conference of the Parties, present to the Conference of the Parties, reports on measures which it has taken for the implementation of the provisions of this Convention and their effectiveness in meeting the objectives of this Convention.

ARTICLE 27
SETTLEMENT OF DISPUTES

1. In the event of a dispute between Contracting Parties concerning the interpretation or application of this Convention, the parties concerned shall seek solution by negotiation.

2. If the Parties concerned cannot reach agreement by negotiation, they may jointly seek the good offices of, or request mediation by, a third party.
3. When ratifying, accepting, approving or acceding to this Convention, or at any time thereafter, a State or regional economic integration organization may declare in writing to the Depositary that for a dispute not resolved in accordance with paragraph 1 or paragraph 2 above, it accepts one or both of the following means of dispute settlement as compulsory:
(a) Arbitration in accordance with the procedure laid down in Part 1 of Annex II;
(b) Submission of the dispute to the International Court of Justice.
4. If the parties to the dispute have not, in accordance with paragraph 3 above, accepted the same or any procedure, the dispute shall be submitted to conciliation in accordance with Part 2 of Annex II unless the parties otherwise agree.
5. The provisions of this Article shall apply with respect to any protocol except as otherwise provided in the protocol concerned.

ARTICLE 28
ADOPTION OF PROTOCOLS
1. The Contracting Parties shall cooperate in the formulation and adoption of protocols to this Convention.
2. Protocols shall be adopted at a meeting of the Conference of the Parties.
3. The text of any proposed protocol shall be communicated to the Contracting Parties by the Secretariat at least six months before such a meeting.

ARTICLE 29
AMENDMENT OF THE CONVENTION OR PROTOCOLS
1. Amendments to this Convention may be proposed by any Contracting Party. Amendments to any protocol may be proposed by any Party to that protocol.
2. Amendments to this Convention shall be adopted at a meeting of the Conference of the Parties. Amendments to any protocol shall be adopted at a meeting of the Parties to the Protocol in question. The text of any proposed amendment to this Convention or to any protocol, except as may otherwise be provided in such protocol, shall be communicated to the Parties to the instrument in question by the secretariat at least six months before the meeting at which it is proposed for adoption. The secretariat shall also communicate proposed amendments to the signatories to this Convention for information.
3. The Parties shall make every effort to reach agreement on any proposed amendment to this Convention or to any protocol by consensus. If all efforts at consensus have been exhausted, and no agreement reached, the amendment shall as a last resort be adopted by a two-thirds majority vote of the Parties to the instrument in question present and voting at the meeting, and shall be submitted by the Depositary to all Parties for ratification, acceptance or approval.
4. Ratification, acceptance or approval of amendments shall be notified to the Depositary in writing. Amendments adopted in accordance with paragraph 3 above shall enter into force among Parties having accepted them on the ninetieth day after the deposit of instruments of ratification, acceptance or approval by at least two thirds of the Contracting Parties to this Convention or of the Parties to the protocol concerned, except as may otherwise be provided in such protocol. Thereafter the amendments shall enter into force for any other Party on the ninetieth day after that Party deposits its instrument of ratification, acceptance or approval of

the amendments.
5. For the purposes of this Article, "Parties present and voting" means Parties present and casting an affirmative or negative vote.

ARTICLE 30
ADOPTION AND AMENDMENT OF ANNEXES

1. The annexes to this Convention or to any protocol shall form an integral part of the Convention or of such protocol, as the case may be, and, unless expressly provided otherwise, a reference to this Convention or its protocols constitutes at the same time a reference to any annexes thereto. Such annexes shall be restricted to procedural, scientific, technical and administrative matters.
2. Except as may be otherwise provided in any protocol with respect to its annexes, the following procedure shall apply to the proposal, adoption and entry into force of additional annexes to this Convention or of annexes to any protocol:
(a) Annexes to this Convention or to any protocol shall be proposed and adopted according to the procedure laid down in Article 29;
(b) Any Party that is unable to approve an additional annex to this Convention or an annex to any protocol to which it is Party shall so notify the Depositary, in writing, within one year from the date of the communication of the adoption by the Depositary. The Depositary shall without delay notify all Parties of any such notification received. A Party may at any time withdraw a previous declaration of objection and the annexes shall thereupon enter into force for that Party subject to subparagraph (c) below;
(c) On the expiry of one year from the date of the communication of the adoption by the Depositary, the annex shall enter into force for all Parties to this Convention or to any protocol concerned which have not submitted a notification in accordance with the provisions of subparagraph (b) above.
3. The proposal, adoption and entry into force of amendments to annexes to this Convention or to any protocol shall be subject to the same procedure as for the proposal, adoption and entry into force of annexes to the Convention or annexes to any protocol.
4. If an additional annex or an amendment to an annex is related to an amendment to this Convention or to any protocol, the additional annex or amendment shall not enter into force until such time as the amendment to the Convention or to the protocol concerned enters into force.

ARTICLE 31
RIGHT TO VOTE

1. Except as provided for in paragraph 2 below, each Contracting Party to this Convention or to any protocol shall have one vote.
2. Regional economic integration organizations, in matters within their competence, shall exercise their right to vote with a number of votes equal to the number of their member States which are Contracting Parties to this Convention or the relevant protocol. Such organizations shall not exercise their right to vote if their member States exercise theirs, and vice versa.

ARTICLE 32
RELATIONSHIP BETWEEN THIS CONVENTION AND ITS PROTOCOLS

1. A State or a regional economic integration organization may not become a Party to a

protocol unless it is, or becomes at the same time, a Contracting Party to this Convention.
2. Decisions under any protocol shall be taken only by the Parties to the protocol concerned. Any Contracting Party that has not ratified, accepted or approved a protocol may participate as an observer in any meeting of the parties to that protocol.

ARTICLE 33
SIGNATURE

This Convention shall be open for signature at Rio de Janeiro by all States and any regional economic integration organization from 5 June 1992 until 14 June 1992, and at the United Nations Headquarters in New York from 15 June 1992 to 4 June 1993.

ARTICLE 34
RATIFICATION, ACCEPTANCE OR APPROVAL

1. This Convention and any protocol shall be subject to ratification, acceptance or approval by States and any regional economic integration organizations. Instruments of ratification, acceptance or approval shall be deposited with the Depositary.
2. Any organization referred to in paragraph 1 above which becomes a Contracting Party to this Convention or any protocol without any of its member States being a Contracting Party shall be bound by all the obligations under the Convention or the protocol, as the case may be. In the case of such organizations, one or more of whose member States is a Contracting Party to this Convention or relevant protocol, the organization and its member States shall decide on their respective responsibilities for the performance of their obligations under the Convention or protocol, as the case may be. In such cases, the organization and the member States shall not be entitled to exercise rights under the Convention or relevant protocol concurrently.
3. In their instruments of ratification, acceptance or approval, the organizations referred to in paragraph 1 above shall declare the extent of their competence with respect to the matters governed by the Convention or the relevant protocol. These organizations shall also inform the Depositary of any relevant modification in the extent of their competence.

ARTICLE 35
ACCESSION

1. This Convention and any protocol shall be open for accession by States and by regional economic integration organizations from the date on which the Convention or the protocol concerned is closed for signature. The instruments of accession shall be deposited with the Depositary.
2. In their instruments of accession, the organizations referred to in paragraph 1 above shall declare the extent of their competence with respect to the matters governed by the Convention or the relevant protocol. These organizations shall also inform the Depositary of any relevant modification in the extent of their competence.
3. The provisions of Article 34, paragraph 2, shall apply to regional economic integration organizations which accede to this Convention or any protocol.

ARTICLE 36
ENTRY INTO FORCE

1. This Convention shall enter into force on the ninetieth day after the date of deposit of the

thirtieth instrument of ratification, acceptance, approval or accession.
2. Any protocol shall enter into force on the ninetieth day after the date of deposit of the number of instruments of ratification, acceptance, approval or accession, specified in that protocol, has been deposited.
3. For each Contracting Party which ratifies, accepts or approves this Convention or accedes thereto after the deposit of the thirtieth instrument of ratification, acceptance, approval or accession, it shall enter into force on the ninetieth day after the date of deposit by such Contracting Party of its instrument of ratification, acceptance, approval or accession.
4. Any protocol, except as otherwise provided in such protocol, shall enter into force for a Contracting Party that ratifies, accepts or approves that protocol or accedes thereto after its entry into force pursuant to paragraph 2 above, on the ninetieth day after the date on which that Contracting party deposits its instrument of ratification, acceptance, approval or accession, or on the date on which this Convention enters into force for that Contracting Party, whichever shall be the later.
5. For the purposes of paragraphs 1 and 2 above, any instrument deposited by a regional economic integration organization shall not be counted as additional to those deposited by member States of such organization.

ARTICLE 37
RESERVATIONS
No reservations may be made to this Convention.

ARTICLE 38
WITHDRAWALS
1. At any time after two years from the date on which this Convention has entered into force for a Contracting Party, that Contracting Party may withdraw from the Convention by giving written notification to the Depositary.
2. Any such withdrawal shall take place upon expiry of one year after the date of its receipt by the Depositary, or on such later date as may be specified in the notification of the withdrawal.
3. Any Contracting Party which withdraws from this Convention shall be considered as also having withdrawn from any protocol to which it is party.

ARTICLE 39
FINANCIAL INTERIM ARRANGEMENTS
Provided that it has been fully restructured in accordance with the requirements of Article 21, the Global Environment Facility of the United Nations Development Programme, the United Nations Environment Programme and the International Bank for Reconstruction and Development shall be the institutional structure referred to in Article 21 on an interim basis, for the period between the entry into force of this Convention and the first meeting of the Conference of the Parties or until the Conference of the Parties decides which institutional structure will be designated in accordance with Article 21.

ARTICLE 40
SECRETARIAT INTERIM ARRANGEMENTS
The secretariat to be provided by the Executive Director of the United Nations Environment

Programme shall be the secretariat referred to in Article 24, paragraph 2, on an interim basis for the period between the entry into force of this Convention and the first meeting of the Conference of the Parties.

ARTICLE 41
DEPOSITARY

The Secretary-General of the United Nations shall assume the functions of Depositary of this Convention and any protocols.

ARTICLE 42
AUTHENTIC TEXTS

The original of this Convention, of which the Arabic, Chinese, English, French, Russian and Spanish texts are equally authentic, shall be deposited with the Secretary-General of the United Nations.

IN WITNESS WHEREOF the undersigned, being duly authorized to that effect, have signed this Convention.

Done at Rio de Janeiro on this fifth day of June, one thousand nine hundred and ninety-two.

ANNEX I
IDENTIFICATION AND MONITORING

1. Ecosystems and habitats: containing high diversity, large numbers of endemic or threatened species, or wilderness; required by migratory species; of social, economic, cultural or scientific importance; or, which are representative, unique or associated with key evolutionary or other biological processes;
2. Species and communities which are: threatened; wild relatives of domesticated or cultivated species; or medicinal, agricultural or other economic value; or social, scientific or cultural importance; or importance for research into the conservation and sustainable use of biological diversity, such as indicator species; and
3. Described genomes and genes of social, scientific or economic importance.

ANNEX II
Part 1

ARBITRATION
ARTICLE 1

The claimant party shall notify the secretariat that the parties are referring a dispute to arbitration pursuant to Article 27. The notification shall state the subject-matter of arbitration and include, in particular, the articles of the Convention or the protocol, the interpretation or application of which are at issue. If the parties do not agree on the subject matter of the dispute before the President of the tribunal is designated, the arbitral tribunal shall determine the subject matter. The secretariat shall forward the information thus received to all Contracting Parties to this Convention or to the protocol concerned.

ARTICLE 2
1. In disputes between two parties, the arbitral tribunal shall consist of three members. Each of the parties to the dispute shall appoint an arbitrator and the two arbitrators so appointed shall designate by common agreement the third arbitrator who shall be the President of the tribunal. The latter shall not be a national of one of the parties to the dispute, nor have his or her usual place of residence in the territory of one of these parties, nor be employed by any of them, nor have dealt with the case in any other capacity.
2. In disputes between more than two parties, parties in the same interest shall appoint one arbitrator jointly by agreement.
3. Any vacancy shall be filled in the manner prescribed for the initial appointment.

ARTICLE 3
1. If the President of the arbitral tribunal has not been designated within two months of the appointment of the second arbitrator, the Secretary-General of the United Nations shall, at the request of a party, designate the President within a further two-month period.
2. If one of the parties to the dispute does not appoint an arbitrator within two months of receipt of the request, the other party may inform the Secretary-General who shall make the designation within a further two-month period.

ARTICLE 4
The arbitral tribunal shall render its decisions in accordance with the provisions of this Convention, any protocols concerned, and international law.

ARTICLE 5
Unless the parties to the dispute otherwise agree, the arbitral tribunal shall determine its own rules of procedure.

ARTICLE 6
The arbitral tribunal may, at the request of one of the parties, recommend essential interim measures of protection.

ARTICLE 7
The parties to the dispute shall facilitate the work of the arbitral tribunal and, in particular, using all means at their disposal, shall:
(a) Provide it with all relevant documents, information and facilities; and
(b) Enable it, when necessary, to call witnesses or experts and receive their evidence.

ARTICLE 8
The parties and the arbitrators are under an obligation to protect the confidentiality of any information they receive in confidence during the proceedings of the arbitral tribunal.

ARTICLE 9
Unless the arbitral tribunal determines otherwise because of the particular circumstances of the

case, the costs of the tribunal shall be borne by the parties to the dispute in equal shares. The tribunal shall keep a record of all its costs, and shall furnish a final statement thereof to the parties.

ARTICLE 10
Any Contracting Party that has an interest of a legal nature in the subject-matter of the dispute which may be affected by the decision in the case, may intervene in the proceedings with the consent of the tribunal.

ARTICLE 11
The tribunal may hear and determine counterclaims arising directly out of the subject-matter of the dispute.

ARTICLE 12
Decisions both on procedure and substance of the arbitral tribunal shall be taken by a majority vote of its members.

ARTICLE 13
If one of the parties to the dispute does not appear before the arbitral tribunal or fails to defend its case, the other party may request the tribunal to continue the proceedings and to make its award. Absence of a party or a failure of a party to defend its case shall not constitute a bar to the proceedings. Before rendering its final decision, the arbitral tribunal must satisfy itself that the claim is well founded in fact and law.

ARTICLE 14
The tribunal shall render its final decisions within five months of the date on which it is fully constituted unless it finds it necessary to extend the time-limit for a period which should be exceed five more months.

ARTICLE 15
The final decision of the arbitral tribunal shall be confined to the subject-matter of the dispute and shall state the reasons on which it is based. It shall contain the names of the members who have participated and the date of the final decision. Any member of the tribunal may attach a separate or dissenting opinion to the final decision.

ARTICLE 16
The award shall be binding on the parties to the dispute. It shall be without appeal unless the parties to the dispute have agreed in advance to an appellate procedure.

ARTICLE 17
Any controversy which may arise between the parties to the dispute as regards the interpretation or manner of implementation of the final decision may be submitted by either party for decision to the arbitral tribunal which rendered it.

UN Convention on Biological Diversity

Part 2
CONCILIATION

ARTICLE 1
A conciliation commission shall be created upon the request of one of the parties to the dispute. The commission shall, unless the parties otherwise agree, be composed of five members, two appointed by each Party concerned and a President chosen jointly by those members.

ARTICLE 2
In disputes between more than two parties, parties in the same interest shall appoint their members of the commission jointly by agreement. Where two or more parties have separate interests or there is a disagreement as to whether they are of the same interest, they shall appoint their members separately.

ARTICLE 3
If any appointments by the parties are not made within two months of the date of the request to create a conciliation commission, the Secretary-General of the United Nations shall, if asked to do so by the party that made the request, make those appointments within a further two-month period.

ARTICLE 4
If a President of the conciliation commission has not been chosen within two months of the last of the members of the commission being appointed, the Secretary-General of the United Nations shall, if asked to do so by a party, designate a President within a further two-month period.

ARTICLE 5
The conciliation commission shall take its decisions by majority vote of its members. It shall, unless the parties to the dispute otherwise agree, determine its own procedure. It shall render a proposal for resolution of the dispute, which the parties shall consider in good faith.

ARTICLE 6
A disagreement as to whether the conciliation commission has competence shall be decided by the commission.

ANNEX 2
UNITED NATIONS FRAMEWORK CONVENTION ON CLIMATE CHANGE

FULL TEXT

The Parties to this Convention

Acknowledge that change in the Earth's climate and its adverse effects are a common concern of humankind,
Concerned that human activities have been substantially increasing the atmospheric concentrations of greenhouse gases, that these increases enhance the natural greenhouse effect, and that this will result on average in an additional warming of the Earth's surface and atmosphere and may adversely affect natural ecosystems and humankind,
Noting that the largest share of historical and current global emissions of greenhouse gases has originated in developed countries, that per capita emissions in developing countries are still relatively low and that the share of global emissions originating in developing countries will grow to meet their social and development needs,
Aware of the role and importance in terrestrial and marine ecosystems of sinks and reservoirs of greenhouse gases,
Noting that there are many uncertainties in predictions of climate change, particularly with regard to the timing, magnitude and regional patterns thereof,
Acknowledge that the global nature of climate change calls for the widest possible cooperation by all countries and their participation in an effective and appropriate international response, in accordance with their common but differentiated responsibilities and respective capabilities and their social and economic conditions,
Recalling the pertinent provisions of the Declaration of the United Nations Conference on the Human Environment, adopted at Stockholm on 16 June 1972,
Recalling also that States have, in accordance with the Charter of the United Nations and the principles of international law, the sovereign right to exploit their own resources pursuant to their own environmental and developmental policies, and the responsibility to ensure that activities within their jurisdiction or control do not cause damage to the environment of other States or of areas beyond the limits of national jurisdiction,
Reaffirming the principle of sovereignty of States in international cooperation to address climate change,
Recognizing that States should enact effective environmental legislation, that environmental standards, management objectives and priorities should reflect the environmental and developmental context to which they apply, and that standards applied by some countries may be inappropriate and of unwarranted economic and social cost to other countries, in particular developing countries,
Recalling the provisions of General Assembly resolution 44/228 of 22 December 1989 on the United Nations Conference on Environment and Development, and resolutions 43/53 of 6 December 1988, 44/207 of 22 December 1989, 45/212 of 21 December 1990 and 46/169 of

19 December 1991 on protection of global climate for present and future generations of mankind,

Recalling also the provisions of General Assembly resolution 44/206 of 22 December 1989 on the possible adverse effects of sea level rise on islands and coastal areas, particularly low-lying coastal areas and the pertinent provisions of General Assembly resolution 44/172 of 19 December 1989 on the implementation of the Plan of Action to Combat Desertification,

Recalling further the Vienna Convention for the Protection of the Ozone Layer, 1985, and the Montreal Protocol on Substances that Deplete the Ozone Layer, 1987, as adjusted and amended on 29 June 1990,

Noting the Ministerial Declaration of the Second World Climate Conference adopted on 7 November 1990,

Conscious of the valuable analytical work being conducted by many States on climate change and of the important contributions of the World Meteorological Organization, the United Nations Environment Programme and other organs, organizations and bodies of the United Nations system, as well as other international and inter-governmental bodies, to the exchange of results of scientific research and the coordination of research,

Recognizing that steps required to understand and address climate change will be environmentally, socially and economically most effective if they are based on relevant scientific, technical and economic considerations and continually re-evaluated in the light of new findings in these area,

Recognizing that various actions to address climate change can be justified economically in their own right and can also help in solving other environmental problems,

Recognizing also the need for developed countries to take immediate action in a flexible manner on the basis of clear priorities, as a first step towards comprehensive response strategies at the global, national and, where agreed, regional levels that take into account all greenhouse gases, with due consideration of their relative contributions to the enhancement of the greenhouse effect,

Recognizing further that low-lying and other small island countries, countries with low-lying coastal, arid and semi-arid areas or areas liable to floods, drought and desertification, and developing countries with fragile mountainous ecosystems are particularly vulnerable to the adverse effects of climate change,

Recognizing the special difficulties of those countries, especially developing countries, whose economies are particularly dependent on fossil fuel production, use and exportation, as a consequence of action taken on limiting greenhouse gas emissions,

Affirming that responses to climate change should be coordinated with social and economic development in an integrated manner with a view to avoiding adverse impacts on the latter, taking into full account the legitimate priority needs of developing countries for the achievement of sustained economic growth and the eradication of poverty,

Recognizing that all countries, especially developing countries, need access to resources required to achieve sustainable social and economic development and that, in order for developing countries to progress towards that goal, their energy consumptions will need to grown taking into account the possibilities for achieving greater energy efficiency and for controlling greenhouse gas emissions in general, including through the application of new technologies on terms which make such an application economically and socially beneficial,

Determined to protect the climate system for present and future generations,

Convention on Climate Change

Have agreed as follows:

ARTICLE 1
DEFINITIONS[1]

For the purposes of this Convention:
1. "Adverse effects of climate change" means changes in the physical environment or biota resulting from climate change which have significant deleterious effects on the composition, resilience or productivity of natural and managed ecosystems or on the operation of socio-economic systems or on human health and welfare.
2. "Climate change" means a change of climate which is attributed directly or indirectly to human activity that alters the composition of the global atmosphere and which is in addition to natural climate variability observed over comparable time periods.
3. "Climate system" means the totality of the atmosphere, hydrosphere, biosphere and geosphere and their interactions.
4. "Emissions" means the release of greenhouse gases and/or their precursors into the atmosphere over a specified area and period of time.
5. "Greenhouse gases" means those gaseous constituents of the atmosphere, both natural and anthropogenic, that absorb and re-emit infrared radiation.
6. "Regional economic integration organization" means an organization constituted by sovereign States of a given region which has competence in respect of matters governed by this Convention or its protocols and has been duly authorized, in accordance with its internal procedures, to sing, ratify, accept, approve or accede to the instruments concerned.
7. "Reservoir" means a component or components of the climate system where a greenhouse gas or a precursor of a greenhouse gas is stored.
8. "Sink" means any process, activity or mechanism which removes a greenhouse gas, an aerosol or a precursor of a greenhouse gas from the atmosphere.
9. "Source" means any process or activity which releases a greenhouse gas, an aerosol or a precursor of a greenhouse gas into the atmosphere.

ARTICLE 2
OBJECTIVE

The ultimate objective of this Convention and any related legal instruments that the Conference of the Parties may adopt is to achieve, in accordance with the relevant provisions of the Convention, stabilization of greenhouse gas concentrations in the atmosphere at a level that would prevent dangerous anthropogenic interference with the climate system. Such a level should be achieved within a time frame sufficient to allow ecosystems to adapt naturally to climate change, to ensure that food production is not threatened and to enable economic development to proceed in a sustainable manner.

ARTICLE 3
PRINCIPLES

In their actions to achieve the objective of the Convention and to implement its provisions, the

---

[1] - Title of articles are included solely to assist the reader.

Parties shall be guided, *inter alia*, by the following:
1. The Parties should protect the climate system for the benefit of present and future generations of humankind, on the basis of equity and in accordance with their common but differentiated responsibilities and respective capabilities. Accordingly, the developed country Parties should take the lead in combating climate change and the adverse effects thereof.
2. The specific needs and special circumstances of developing country Parties, especially those that are particularly vulnerable to the adverse effects of climate change, and of those Parties, especially developing country Parties, that would have to bear a disproportionate or abnormal burden under the Convention, should be given full consideration.
3. The Parties should take precautionary measures to anticipate, prevent or minimize the causes of climate change and mitigate its adverse effects. Where there are threats of serious or irreversible damage, lack of full scientific certainty should not be used as a reason for postponing such measures, taking into account that policies and measures to deal with climate change should be cost-effective so as to ensure global benefits at the lowest possible cost. To achieve this, such policies and measures should take into account different socio-economic contexts, be comprehensive, cover all relevant sources, sinks and reservoirs of greenhouse gases and adaptation, and comprise all economic sectors. Efforts to address climate change may be carried out cooperatively by interested Parties.
4. The Parties have a right to, and should, promote sustainable development. Policies and measures to protect the climate system against human-induced change should be appropriate for the specific conditions of each Party and should be integrated with national development programmes, taking into account that economic development is essential for adopting measures to address climate change.
5. The Parties should cooperate to promote a supportive and open international economic system that would lead to sustainable economic growth and development in all Parties, particularly developing country Parties, thus enabling them better to address the problems of climate change. Measures taken to combat climate change, including unilateral ones, should not constitute a means of arbitrary or unjustifiable discrimination or a disguised restriction on international trade.

ARTICLE 4
COMMITMENTS
1. All Parties, taking into account their common but differentiated responsibilities and their specific national and regional development priorities, objectives and circumstances, shall:
   (a) Develop, periodically update, publish and make available to the Conference of the Parties, in accordance with Article 12, national inventories or anthropogenic emissions by sources and removals by sinks of all greenhouse gases not controlled by the Montreal Protocol, using comparable methodologies to be agreed upon by the Conference of the Parties;
   (b) Formulate, implement, publish and regularly update national and, where appropriate, regional programmes containing measures to mitigate climate change by addressing anthropogenic emissions by sources and removals by sinks of all greenhouse gases not controlled by the Montreal Protocol, and measures to facilitate adequate adaptation to climate change;
   (c) Promote and cooperate in the development, application and diffusion, including transfer, of technologies, practices and processes that control, reduce or prevent anthropogenic emissions of greenhouse gases not controlled by the Montreal Protocol

in all relevant sectors, including the energy, transport, industry, agriculture, forestry and waste management sectors;

(d) Promote sustainable management, and promote and cooperate in the conservation and enhancement, as appropriate, of sinks and reservoirs of all greenhouse gases not controlled by the Montreal Protocol, including biomass, forests and oceans as well as other terrestrial, coastal and marine ecosystems;

(e) Cooperate in preparing for adaptation to the impacts of climate change; develop and elaborate appropriate and integrated plans for coastal zone management, water resources and agriculture, and for the protection and rehabilitation of areas, particularly in Africa, affected by drought and desertification, as well as floods;

(f) Take climate change considerations into account, to the extent feasible, in their relevant social, economic and environmental policies and actions, and employ appropriate methods, for example impact assessments, formulated and determined nationally, with a view to minimizing adverse effects on the economy, on public health and on the quality of the environment, of projects or measures undertaken by them to mitigate or adapt to climate change;

(g) Promote and cooperate in scientific, technological, technical, socio-economic and other research, systematic observations and development of data archives related to the climate system and intended to further the understanding and to reduce or eliminate the remaining uncertainties regarding the causes, effects, magnitude and timing of climate change and the economic and social consequences of various response strategies;

(h) Promote and cooperate in the full, open and prompt exchange of relevant scientific, technological, technical, socio-economic and legal information related to the climate system and climate change, and to the economic and social consequences of various response strategies;

(i) Promote and cooperate in education, training and public awareness related to climate change and encourage the widest participation in this process, including that of non-governmental organizations; and

(j) Communicate to the Conference of the Parties information related to implementation, in accordance with Article 12.

2. The developed country Parties and other Parties included in annex 1 commit themselves specifically as provided for in the following:

(a) Each of these Parties shall adopt national[1]/policies and take corresponding measures on the mitigation of climate change, by limiting its anthropogenic emissions of greenhouse gases and protecting and enhancing its greenhouse gas sinks and reservoirs. These policies and measures will demonstrate that developed countries are taking the lead in modifying longer-term trends in anthropogenic emissions consistent with the objective of the Convention, recognizing that the return by the end of the present decade to earlier levels of anthropogenic emissions of carbon dioxide and other greenhouse gases not controlled by the Montreal Protocol would contribute to such modification, and taking into account the differences in these Parties' starting points

---

[1] - This includes policies and measures adopted by regional economic integration organizations.

and approaches, economic structures and resource bases, the need to maintain strong and sustainable economic growth, available technologies and other individual circumstances, as well as the need for equitable and appropriate contribution by each of these Parties to the global effort regarding that objective. These Parties may implement such policies and measures jointly with other Parties and may assist other Parties in contributing to the achievement of the objective of the Convention and, in particular, that of this subparagraph;

(b) In order to promote progress to this end, each of these Parties shall communicate, within six months of the entry into force of the Convention for it and periodically thereafter, and in accordance with Article 12, detailed information on its policies and measures referred to in subparagraph (a) above, as well as on its resulting projected anthropogenic emissions by sources and removals by sinks of greenhouse gases not controlled by the Montreal Protocol for the period referred to in subparagraph (a), with the aim of returning individually or jointly to their 1990 levels these anthropogenic emissions of carbon dioxide and other greenhouse gases not controlled by the Montreal Protocol. This information will be reviewed by the Conference of the Parties, at its first session and periodically thereafter, in accordance with Article 7;

(c) Calculations of emissions by sources and removals by sinks of greenhouse gases for the purposes of subparagraph (b) above should take into account the best available scientific knowledge, including of the effective capacity of sinks and the respective contributions of such gases to climate change. The Conference of the Parties shall consider and agree on methodologies for these calculations at its first session and review them regularly thereafter;

(d) The Conference of the Parties shall, at its first session, review the adequacy of subparagraphs (a) and (b) above. Such review shall be carried out in the light of the best available scientific information and assessment on climate change and its impacts, as well as relevant technical, social and economic information. Based on the review, the Conference of the Parties shall take appropriate action, which may include the adoption of amendments to the commitments in subparagraphs (a) and (b) above. The Conference of the Parties, at its first sessions, shall also take decisions regarding criteria for joint implementation as indicated in subparagraph (a) above. A second review of subparagraphs (a) and (b) shall take place not later than 31 December 1998, and thereafter at regular intervals determined by the Conference of the Parties, until the objective of the Convention is met;

(e) Each of these Parties shall:
    (i) coordinate as appropriate with other such Parties, relevant economic and administrative instruments developed to achieve the objective of the Convention; and
    (ii) identify and periodically review its own policies and practices which encourage activities that lead to greater levels of anthropogenic emissions of greenhouse gases not controlled by the Montreal Protocol than would otherwise occur;

(f) The Conference of the Parties shall review, not later than 31 December 1998, available information with a view to taking decisions regarding such amendments to the lists in annexes I and II as may be appropriate, with the approval of the Party concerned;

Convention on Climate Change

(g) Any Party not included in annex I may, in its instrument of ratification, acceptance, approval or accession, or at any time thereafter, notify the Depositary that it intends to be bound by subparagraphs (a) and (b) above. The Depositary shall inform the other signatories and Parties of any such notification.

3. The developed country Parties and other developed Parties included in annex II shall provide new and additional financial resources to meet the agreed full costs incurred by developing country Parties in complying with their obligations under Article 12, paragraph 1. They shall also provide such financial resources, including for the transfer of technology, needed by the developing country Parties to meet the agreed full incremental costs of implementing measures that are covered by paragraph 1 of this Article and that are agreed between a developing country Party and the international entity or entities referred to in Article 11, in accordance with that Article. The implementation of these commitments shall take into account the need for adequacy and predictability in the flow of funds and the importance of appropriate burden sharing among the developed country Parties.

4. The developed country Parties and other developed Parties included in annex II shall also assist the developing country Parties that are particularly vulnerable to the adverse effects of climate change in meeting costs of adaptation to those adverse effects.

5. The developed country Parties and other developed Parties included in annex II shall take all practicable steps to promote, facilitate and finance, as appropriate, the transfer of, or access to, environmentally sound technologies and know-how to other Parties, particularly developing country Parties, to enable them to implement the provisions of the Convention. In this process, the developed country Parties shall support the development and enhancement of endogenous capacities and technologies of developing country Parties. Other Parties and organizations in a position to do so may also assist in facilitating the transfer of such technologies.

6. In the implementation of their commitments under paragraph 2 above, a certain degree of flexibility shall be allowed by the Conference of the Parties to the Parties included in annex I undergoing the process of transition to a market economy, in order to enhance the ability of these parties to address climate change, including with regard to the historical level of anthropogenic emissions of greenhouse gases not controlled by the Montreal Protocol chosen as a reference.

7. The extent to which developing country Parties will effectively implement their commitment under the Convention will depend on the effective implementation by developed country Parties of their commitments under the Convention related to financial resources and transfer of technology and will take fully into account that economic and social development and poverty eradication are the first and overriding priorities of the developing country Parties.

8. In the implementation of the commitments in this Article, the Parties shall give full consideration to what actions are necessary under the Convention, including actions related to funding, insurance and the transfer of technology, to meet the specific needs and concerns of developing country Parties arising from the adverse effects of climate change and/or the impact of the implementation of response measures, especially on:

(a) Small island countries;
(b) Countries with low-lying coastal areas;
(c) Countries with arid and semi-arid areas, forested areas and areas liable to forest decay;
(d) Countries with areas prone to natural disasters;

(e) Countries with areas liable to drought and desertification;
(f) Countries with areas of high urban atmospheric pollution;
(g) Countries with areas with fragile ecosystems, including mountainous ecosystems;
(h) Countries whose ecosystems are highly dependent on income generated from the production, processing and export, and/or on consumption of fossil fuels and associated energy-intensive products; and
(i) Land-locked and transit countries.

Further, the Conference of the Parties may take actions, as appropriate, with respect to this paragraph.

9. The Parties shall take full account of the specific needs and special situations of the least developed countries in their actions with regard to funding and transfer of technology.

10. The Parties shall, in accordance with Article 10, take into consideration in the implementation of the commitments of the Convention the situation of Parties, particularly developing country Parties, with economies that are vulnerable to the adverse effects of the implementation of measures to respond to climate change. This applies notably to Parties with economies that are highly dependent on income generated from the production, processing and export, and/or consumption of fossil fuels and associated energy-intensive products and/or the use of fossil fuels for which such Parties have serious difficulties in switching to alternatives.

ARTICLE 5
RESEARCH AND SYSTEMATIC OBSERVATION

In carrying out their commitments under Article 4, paragraph 1(g), the Parties shall:
(a) Support and further develop, as appropriate international and intergovernmental programmes and networks or organizations aimed at defining, conducting, assessing and financing research, data collection and systematic observation, taking into account the need to minimize duplication or effort;
(b) Support international and intergovernmental efforts to strengthen systematic observation and national scientific and technical research capacities and capabilities, particularly in developing countries, and to promote access to, and the exchange of, data and analyses thereof obtained from areas beyond national jurisdiction; and
(c) Take into account the particular concerns and needs of developing countries and cooperate in improving their endogenous capacities and capabilities to participate in the efforts referred to in subparagraphs (a) and (b) above.

ARTICLE 6
EDUCATION, TRAINING AND PUBLIC AWARENESS

In carrying out their commitments under Article 4, paragraph 1(i), the Parties shall:
(a) Promote and facilitate at the national and, as appropriate, subregional and regional levels, and in accordance with national laws and regulations, and within their respective capacities:
  (i) the development and implementation of educational and public awareness programmes on climate change and its effects;
  (ii) public access to information on climate change and its effects;
  (iii) public participation in addressing climate change and its effects and developing adequate responses; and
  (iv) training of scientific, technical and managerial personnel.
(b) Cooperate in and promote, at the international level, and, where appropriate, using existing bodies:

(i) the development and exchange of educational and public awareness material on climate change and its effects; and
(ii) the development and implementation of education and training programmes, including the strengthening of national institutions and the exchange or secondment of personnel to train experts in this field, in particular for developing countries.

ARTICLE 7
CONFERENCE OF THE PARTIES

1. A Conference of the Parties is hereby established.
2. The Conference of the Parties, as the supreme body of this Convention, shall keep under regular review the implementation of the Convention and any related legal instruments that the Conference of the Parties may adopt, and shall make, within its mandate, the decisions necessary to promote the effective implementation of the Convention. To this end, it shall:
    (a) Periodically examine the obligations of the Parties and the institutional arrangements under the Convention, in the light of the objective of the Convention, the experience gained in its implementation and the evolution of scientific and technological knowledge;
    (b) Promote and facilitate the exchange of information on measures adopted by the Parties to address climate change and its effects, taking into account the differing circumstances, responsibilities and capabilities of the Parties and their respective commitments under the Convention;
    (c) Facilitate, at the request of two of more Parties, the coordination of measures adopted by them to address climate change and its effects, taking into account the differing circumstances, responsibilities and capabilities of the Parties and their respective commitments under the Convention.
    (d) Promote and guide, in accordance with the objectives and provisions of the Convention, the development and periodic refinement of comparable methodologies, to be agreed on by the Conference of the Parties, inter alia, for preparing inventories of greenhouse gas emissions by sources and removals by sinks, and for evaluating the effectiveness of measures to limit the emissions and enhance the removals of these gases;
    (e) Assess, on the basis of all information made available to it in accordance with the provisions of the Convention, the implementation of the Convention by the Parties, the overall effects of the measures taken pursuant to the Convention, in particular environmental, economic and social effects as well as their cumulative impacts and the extent to which progress towards the objectives of the Convention is being achieved;
    (f) Consider and adopt regular reports on the implementation of the Convention and ensure their publication;
    (g) Make recommendations on any matters necessary for the implementation of the Convention;
    (h) Seek to mobilize financial resources in accordance with Article 4, paragraphs 3, 4 and 5, and Article 11;
    (i) Establish such subsidiary bodies as are deemed necessary for the implementation of the Convention;
    (j) Review reports submitted by its subsidiary bodies and provide guidance to them;

(k) Agree upon and adopt, by consensus, rules of procedure and financial rules for itself and for any subsidiary bodies;

(l) Seek and utilize, where appropriate, the services and cooperation of, and information provided by, competent international organizations and intergovernmental and non-governmental bodies; and

(m) Exercise such other functions as are required for the achievement of the objectives of the Convention as well as all other functions assigned to it under the Convention.

3. The Conference of the Parties shall, at its first session, adopt its own rules of procedure as well as those of the subsidiary bodies established by the Convention, which shall include decision-making procedures for matters not already covered by decision-making procedures stipulated in the Convention. Such procedures may include specified majorities required for the adoption of particular decisions.

4. The first session of the Conference of the Parties shall be convened by the interim secretariat referred to in Article 21 and shall take place not later than one year after the date of entry into force of the Convention. Thereafter, ordinary sessions of the Conference of the Parties shall be held every year unless otherwise decided by the Conference of the Parties.

5. Extraordinary sessions of the Conference of the Parties shall be held at such times as may be deemed necessary by the Conference, or at the written request of any Party, provided that, within six months of the request being communicated to the Parties by the secretariat, it is supported by at least one-third of the Parties.

6. The United Nations, its specialized agencies and the International Atomic Energy Agency, as well as any State member thereof or observers thereto not Party to the Convention, may be represented at sessions of the Conference of the Parties as observers. Any body or agency, whether national or international, governmental or non-governmental, which is qualified in matters covered by the Convention, and which has informed the secretariat of its wish to be represented at a session of the Conference of the Parties as an observer, may be so admitted unless at least one-third of the Parties present object. The admission and participation of observers shall be subject to the rules of procedure adopted by the Conference of the Parties.

ARTICLE 8
SECRETARIAT

1. A secretariat is hereby established.
2. The functions of the secretariat shall be:
   (a) To make arrangements for sessions of the Conference of the Parties and its subsidiary bodies established under the Convention and to provide them with services as required;
   (b) To compile and transmit reports submitted to it;
   (c) To facilitate assistance to the Parties, particularly developing country Parties, on request, in the compilation and communication of information required in accordance with the provisions of the Convention;
   (d) To prepare reports on its activities and present them to the Conference of the Parties;
   (e) To ensure the necessary coordination with the secretariat of other relevant international bodies;
   (f) To enter, under the overall guidance of the Conference of the Parties, into such administrative and contractual arrangements as may be required for the effective discharge of its functions; and
   (g) To perform the other secretariat functions specified in the Convention and in any of

its protocols an such other functions as may be determined by the Conference of the Parties.

3. The Conference of the Parties, at its first session, shall designate a permanent secretariat and make arrangements for its functioning.

ARTICLE 9
SUBSIDIARY BODY FOR SCIENTIFIC AND TECHNOLOGICAL ADVICE

1. A subsidiary body for scientific and technological advice is hereby established to provide the Conference of the Parties and, as appropriate, its other subsidiary bodies with timely information and advice on scientific and technological matters relating to the Convention. This body shall be open to participation by all Parties and shall be multidisciplinary. It shall comprise government representatives competent in the relevant field of expertise. It shall report regularly to the Conference of the Parties on all aspects of its work.

2. Under the guidance of the Conference of the Parties, and drawing upon existing competent international bodies, this body shall:
   (a) Provide assessments of the state of scientific knowledge relating to climate change and its effects;
   (b) Prepare scientific assessments on the effects of measures taken in the implementation of the Convention;
   (c) Identify innovative, efficient and state-of-the-art technologies and know-how and advise on the ways and means of promoting development and/or transferring such technologies;
   (d) Provide advice on scientific programmes, international cooperation in research and development related to climate change, as well as on ways and means of supporting endogenous capacity-building in developing countries; and
   (e) Respond to scientific, technological and methodological questions that the Conference of the Parties and its subsidiary bodies may put to the body.

3. The functions and terms of reference of this body may be further elaborated by the Conference of the Parties.

ARTICLE 10
SUBSIDIARY BODY FOR IMPLEMENTATION

1. A subsidiary body for implementation is hereby established to assist the Conference of the Parties in the assessment and review of the effective implementation of the Convention. This body shall be open to participation by all Parties and comprise government representatives who are experts on matters related to climate change. It shall report regularly to the Conference of the Parties on all aspects of its work.

2. Under the guidance of the Conference of the Parties, this body shall:
   (a) Consider the information communicated in accordance with Article 12, paragraph 1, to assess the overall aggregated effect of the steps taken by the Parties in the light of the latest scientific assessments concerning climate change;
   (b) Consider the information communicated in accordance with Article 12, paragraph 2, in order to assist the Conference of the Parties in carrying out the reviews required by Article 4, paragraph 2(d); and
   (c) Assist the Conference of the Parties, as appropriate, in the preparation and

implementation of its decisions.

ARTICLE 11
FINANCIAL MECHANISM

1. A mechanism for the provision of financial resources on a grant or concessional basis, including for the transfer of technology, is hereby defined. It shall function under the guidance of and be accountable to the Conference of the Parties, which shall decide on its policies, programme priorities and eligibility criteria related to this Convention. Its operation shall be entrusted to one or more existing international entities.

2. The financial mechanism shall have an equitable and balanced representation of all Parties within a transparent system of governance.

3. The Conference of the Parties and the entity or entities entrusted with the operation of the financial mechanism shall agree upon arrangements to give effect to the above paragraphs, which shall include the following:

   (a) Modalities to ensure that the funded projects to address climate change are in conformity with the policies, programme priorities and eligibility criteria established by the Conference of the Parties;

   (b) Modalities by which a particular funding decision may be reconsidered in light of these policies, programme priorities and eligibility criteria;

   (c) Provision by the entity or entities of regular reports to the Conference of the Parties on its funding operations, which is consistent with the requirement for accountability set out in paragraph 1 above; and

   (d) Determination in a predictable and identifiable manner of the amount of funding necessary and available for the implementation of this Convention and the conditions under which that amount shall be periodically reviewed.

4. The Conference of the Parties shall make arrangements to implement the above mentioned provisions at its first session, reviewing and taking into account the interim arrangements referred to in Article 21, paragraph 3, and shall decide whether these interim arrangements shall be maintained. Within four years thereafter, the Conference of the Parties shall review the financial mechanism and take appropriate measures.

5. The developed country Parties may also provide and developing country Parties avail themselves of, financial resources related to the implementation of the Convention through bilateral, regional and other multilateral channels.

ARTICLE 12
COMMUNICATION OF INFORMATION RELATED TO IMPLEMENTATION

1. In accordance with Article 4, paragraph 1, each Party shall communicate to the Conference of the Parties, through the secretariat, the following elements of information:

   (a) A national inventory of anthropogenic emissions by sources and removals by sinks of all greenhouse gases not controlled by the Montreal Protocol, to the extent its capacities permit, using comparable methodologies to be promoted and agreed upon by the Conference of the Parties;

   (b) A general description of steps taken or envisaged by the Party to implement the Convention; and

   (c) Any other information that the Party considers relevant to the achievement of the objective of the Convention and suitable for inclusion in its communication, including, if feasible, material relevant for calculations of global emission trends.

Convention on Climate Change

2. Each developed country Party and each other Party included in annex I shall incorporate in its communication the following elements of information:
   (a) A detailed description of the policies and measures that it has adopted to implement its commitment under Article 4, paragraphs 2(a) and 2(b); and
   (b) A specific estimate of the effects that the policies and measures referred to in subparagraph (a) immediately above will have on anthropogenic emissions by its sources and removals by its sinks of greenhouse gases during the period referred to in Article 4, paragraph 2(a).
3. In addition, each developed country Party and each other developed Party included in annex II shall incorporate details of measures taken in accordance with Article 4, paragraphs 3, 4 and
4. Developing country Parties may, on a voluntary basis, propose projects for financing, including specific technologies, materials, equipment, techniques or practices that would be needed to implement such projects, along with, if possible, an estimate of all incremental costs, of the reductions of emissions and increments of removals of greenhouse gases, as well as an estimate of the consequent benefits.
5. Each developed country Party and each other Party included in annex I shall make its initial communication within six months of the entry into force of the Convention for that Party. Each Party not so listed shall make its initial communication within three years of the entry into force of the Convention for that Party, or of the availability of financial resources in accordance with Article 4, paragraph 3. Parties that are at least developed countries may make their initial communication at their discretion. The frequency of subsequent communications by all Parties shall be determined by the Conference of the Parties, taking into account the differentiated timetable set by this paragraph.
6. Information communicated by Parties under this Article shall be transmitted by the secretariat as soon as possible to the Conference of the Parties and to any subsidiary bodies concerned. If necessary, the procedures for the communication of information may be further considered by the Conference of the Parties.
7. From its first session, the Conference of the Parties shall arrange for the provision to developing country Parties of technical and financial support, on request, in compiling and communicating information under this Article, as well as in identifying the technical and financial needs associated with proposed projects and response measures under Article 4. Such support may be provided by other Parties, by competent international organizations and by the secretariat, as appropriate.
8. Any group of Parties may, subject to guidelines adopted by the Conference of the Parties, and to prior notification to the Conference of the Parties, make a joint communication in fulfilment of their obligations under this Article, provided that such a communication includes information on the fulfilment by each of these Parties of its individual obligations under the Convention.
9. Information received by the secretariat that is designated by a Party as confidential, in accordance with criteria to be established by the Conference of the Parties, shall be aggregated by the secretariat to protect its confidentiality before being made available to any of the bodies involved in the communication and review of information.
10. Subject to paragraph 9 above, and without prejudice to the ability of any Party to make public its communication at any time, the secretariat shall make communications by Parties under this Article publicly available at the time they are submitted to the Conference of the

Parties.

ARTICLE 13
RESOLUTION OF QUESTIONS REGARDING IMPLEMENTATION

The Conference of the Parties shall, at its first session, consider the establishment of a multilateral consultative process, available to Parties on their request, for the resolution of questions regarding the implementation of the Convention.

ARTICLE 14
SETTLEMENT OF DISPUTES

1. In the event of a dispute between any two or more Parties concerning the interpretation or application of the Convention, the Parties concerned shall seek a settlement of the dispute through negotiation or any other peaceful means of their own choice.
2. When ratifying, accepting, approving or acceding to the Convention, or at any time thereafter, a Party which is not a regional economic integration organization may declare in a written instrument submitted to the Depositary that, in respect of any dispute concerning the interpretation or application of the Convention, it recognizes as compulsory ipso facto and without special agreement, in relation to any party accepting the same obligation:
    (a) Submission of the dispute to the International Court of Justice, and/or
    (b) Arbitration in accordance with procedures to be adopted by the Conference of the Parties as soon as practicable, in an annex on arbitration.

A Party which is a regional economic integration organization may make a declaration with like effect in relation to arbitration in accordance with the procedures referred to in subparagraph (b) above.

3. A declaration made under paragraph 2 above shall remain in force until it expires in accordance with its terms or until three months after written notice of its revocation has been deposited with the Depositary.
4. A new declaration, a notice of revocation or the expiry of a declaration shall not in any way affect proceedings pending before the International Court of Justice or the arbitral tribunal, unless the parties to the dispute otherwise agree.
5. Subject to the operation of paragraph 2 above, if after twelve months following notification by one Party to another that a dispute exists between them, the Parties concerned have not been able to settle their dispute through the means mentioned in paragraph 1 above, the dispute shall be submitted, at the request of any of the parties to the dispute, to conciliation.
6. A conciliation commission shall be created upon the request of one of the parties to the dispute. The commission shall be composed of an equal number of members appointed by each party concerned and a chairman chosen jointly by the members appointed by each party. The commission shall render a recommendatory award, which the parties shall consider in good faith.
7. Additional procedures relating to conciliation shall be adopted by the Conference of the Parties, as soon as practicable, in an annex on conciliation.
8. The provisions of this Article shall apply to any related legal instrument which the Conference of the Parties may adopt, unless the instrument provides otherwise.

ARTICLE 15
AMENDMENTS TO THE CONVENTION

1. Any Party may propose amendments to the Convention.

2. Amendments to the Convention shall be adopted at an ordinary session of the Conference of the Parties. The text of any proposed amendment to the Convention shall be communicated to the Parties by the secretariat at least six months before the meeting at which it is proposed for adoption. The secretariat shall also communicate proposed amendments to the signatories to the Convention and, for information, to the Depositary.
3. The Parties shall make every effort to reach agreement on any proposed amendment to the Convention by consensus. If all efforts at consensus have been exhausted, and no agreement reached, the amendment shall as a last resort be adopted by a three-fourths majority vote of the Parties present and voting at the meeting. The adopted amendment shall be communicated by the secretariat to the Depositary, who shall circulate it to all Parties for their acceptance.
4. Instruments of acceptance in respect of an amendment shall be deposited with the Depositary. An amendment adopted in accordance with paragraph 3 above shall enter into force for those Parties having accepted it on the ninetieth day after the date of receipt by the Depositary of an instrument of acceptance by at least three-fourths of the Parties to the Convention.
5. The amendment shall enter into force for any other Party on the ninetieth day after the date on which that Party deposits with the Depositary its instrument of acceptance of the said amendment.
6. For the purposes of this Article, "Parties present and voting" means Parties present and casting an affirmative or negative vote.

ARTICLE 16
ADOPTION AND AMENDMENT OF ANNEXES TO THE CONVENTION

1. Annexes to the convention shall form an integral part thereof and, unless otherwise expressly provided, a reference to the convention constitutes at the same time a reference to any annexes thereto. Without prejudice to the provisions of article 14, paragraphs 2(b) and 7, such annexes shall be restricted to lists, forms and any other material of a descriptive nature that is of a scientific, technical, procedural or administrative character.
2. Annexes to the Convention shall be proposed and adopted in accordance with the procedure set forth in Article 15, paragraphs 2, 3 and 4.
3. An annex that has been adopted in accordance with paragraph 2 above shall enter into force for all Parties to the Convention six months after the date of the communication by the Depositary to such Parties of the adoption of the annex, except for those Parties that have notified the Depositary in writing, within that period of their no-acceptance of the annex. The annex shall enter into force for Parties which withdraw their notification of no-acceptance on the ninetieth day after the date on which withdrawal of such notification has been received by the Depositary.
4. The proposal, adoption and entry into force of amendments to annexes to the Convention shall be subject to the same procedure as that for the proposal, adoption and entry into force of annexes to the Convention in accordance with paragraphs 2 and 3 above.
5. If the adoption of an annex or an amendment to an annex involves an amendment to the Convention, that annex or amendment to an annex shall not enter into force until such time as the amendment to the Convention enters into force.

ARTICLE 17
PROTOCOLS

1. The Conference of the parties may, at any ordinary session, adopt protocols to the Convention.
2. The text of any proposed protocol shall be communicated to the Parties by the secretariat at least six months before such a session.
3. The requirements for the entry into force of any protocol shall be established by that instrument.
4. Only Parties to the Convention may be Parties to a protocol.
5. Decisions under any protocol shall be taken only by the Parties to the protocol concerned.

ARTICLE 18
RIGHT TO VOTE

1. Each Party to the convention shall have one vote, except as provided for in paragraph 2 below.
2. Regional economic integration organizations, in matters within their competence, shall exercise their right to vote with a number of votes equal to the number of their member States that are Parties to the Convention. Such an organization shall not exercise its right to vote if any of its member States exercises its right, and vice versa.

ARTICLE 19
DEPOSITARY

The Secretary-General of the United Nations shall be the Depositary of the Convention and of protocols adopted in accordance with Article 17.

ARTICLE 20
SIGNATURE

This Convention shall be open for signature by States Members of the United Nations or of any of its specialized agencies or that are Parties to the Statute of the International Court of Justice and by regional economic integration organizations at Rio de Janeiro, during the United Nations Conference on Environment and Development, and thereafter at United Nations Headquarters in New York from 20 June 1992 to 19 June 1993.

ARTICLE 21
INTERIM ARRANGEMENTS

1. The secretariat functions referred to in Article 8 will be carried out on an interim basis by the secretariat established by the General Assembly of the United Nations in its resolution 45/212 of 21 December 1990, until the completion of the first session of the Conference of the Parties.
2. The head of the interim secretariat referred to in paragraph 1 above will cooperate closely with the Intergovernmental Panel on Climate Change to ensure that the Panel can respond to the need for objective scientific and technical advice. Other relevant scientific bodies could also be consulted.
3. The Global Environment Facility of the United Nations Development Programme, the United Nations Environment Programme and the International Bank for Reconstruction and Development shall be the international entity entrusted with the operation of the financial

mechanism referred to in Article 11 on an interim basis. In this connection, the Global Environment Facility should be appropriately restructured and its membership made universal to enable it to fulfill the requirements of Article 11.

ARTICLE 22
RATIFICATION, ACCEPTANCE, APPROVAL OR ACCESSION

1. The Convention shall be subject to ratification, acceptance, approval or accession by States and by regional economic integration organizations. It shall be open for accession from the day after the date on which the Convention is closed for signature. Instruments of ratification, acceptance, approval or accession shall be deposited with the Depositary.
2. Any regional economic integration organization which becomes a Party to the Convention without any of its member States being a Party shall be bound by all the obligations under the Convention. In the case of such organizations, one or more of whose member States is a Party to the Convention, the organization and its member States shall decide on their respective responsibilities for the performance of their obligations under the Convention. In such cases, the organization and the member States shall not be entitled to exercise rights under the Convention concurrently.
3. In their instruments of ratification, acceptance, approval or accession, regional economic integration organizations shall declare the extent of their competence with respect to the matters governed by the Convention. These organizations shall also inform the Depositary, who shall in turn inform the Parties, of any substantial modification in the extent of their competence.

ARTICLE 23
ENTRY INTO FORCE

1. The Convention shall enter into force on the ninetieth day after the date of deposit of the fiftieth instrument of ratification, acceptance, approval or accession.
2. For each State or regional economic integration organization that ratifies, accepts or approves the Convention or accedes thereto after the deposit of the fiftieth instrument of ratification, acceptance, approval or accession, the Convention shall enter into force on the ninetieth day after the date of deposit by such State or regional economic integration organization of its instrument of ratification, acceptance, approval or accession.
3. For the purposes of paragraphs 1 and 2 above, any instrument deposited by a regional economic integration organization shall not be counted as additional to those deposited by States members of the organization.

ARTICLE 24
RESERVATIONS

No reservations may be made to the Convention.

ARTICLE 25
WITHDRAWAL

1. At any time after three years from the date on which the Convention has entered into force for a Party, that Party may withdraw from the Convention by giving written notification to the Depositary.
2. Any such withdrawal shall take effect upon expiry of one year from the date of receipt by

the Depositary of the notification of withdrawal, or on such later date as may be specified in the notification of withdrawal.

3. Any Party that withdraws from the Convention shall be considered as also having withdrawn from any protocol to which it is a Party.

ARTICLE 26
AUTHENTIC TEXTS

The original of this Convention, of which the Arabic, Chinese, English, French, Russian and Spanish texts are equally authentic, shall be deposited with the Secretary-General of the United Nations.

IN WITNESS WHEREOF the undersigned, being duly authorized to that effect, have signed this Convention.

DONE at New York this ninth day of May one thousand nine hundred and ninety-two.

INDEX

Acid Rain 11, 57,
Acts
. Civil Aviation - (1962) 44
. Clean Air - (1993) 15
. Consumers Protection - (1987) 34, 40
. Conservation of Seal - (1970) 20, 21
. Control of Pollution - (1974, 1989) 24, 33, 44
. Employment Protection - (1978) 11
. Employer's Liability - (1969) 11,34
. EPA (1990) 20, 21, 22, 23, 24
. Factories - (1937, 1961) 11
. Fire Safety of Places of Sports - (1987) 34
. Fish - (1981) 21
. Food and Environment Protection - (1985) 20
. Food Safety - (1990) 38
. Health & Safety at Work - (Compulsory Insurance) (1974) 11
. Medicine - (1974) 19, 38, 68
. Mines & Quarries - (1954) 34
. Misuse of Drugs - (1971) 38
. National Parks and Access to Country - (1949) 20, 21
. Nature Conservation - (1984) 21
. Occupiers Liability - (1957) 34
. Planning & Compensation - (PCA) - 31
. Prevention of Pollution - (1971) 44
. Protection of Birds - (1954) 20
. Public Health - (1961) 33
. Radioactive Materials - (1991) 44
. Radioactive Substances - (1961)
. Reservoirs - (1978, 1981) 45
. Rivers, Pollution - (Protection and Prevention) (1957, 1961, 1989) 33
. Road Traffic - (1988) 44
. Salmon and Fresh Water Fishes - (1975) 21
. Scotland - (1991) 20
. Sea Fish Industry - (1938) 21
. Seal Fisheries (North Pacific) - (1895, 1912) 21
. Shop - (1950) 11
. Town and Countryside (Compensation) - (1991) 24
. Town and Countryside Planning (Hazardous Substances) - (1965, 1971, 1990) 24, 31
. Water - (1972, 1981, 1987, 1989) 11, 20, 33, 44
. Water Industry - (1991) 45
. Whaling Industry Regulations - (1934) 21
. Wildlife and Countryside Protection - (1981) 20, 21

. Wildlife Conservation - (1992) 20, 21
Advisory Panel on Food Security 39
Agenda 21, 51, 52, 53, 62, 63, 64, 90
Albania 15,
Aristotle 6, 22
Atmosphere 12, 61, 67
Arbitration 78, 79, 80
Australia 41

Bhopal Disaster (India) 63
Bible 7
 (New Testament)
   Jesus 7, 8
   John 7
   Paul 7
 (Old Testament)
   Issiah 7
   Jermiah 7
   Leviticus 7
   Psalm 7
Biotechnology 54
British Steel 26, 31, 32

Canada 15
Case(s)
. CA. Adams v Southern Electricity Board (1993) 33
. CA. Regina v Avon County Council Ex parte Tery Adams Ltd (1994) 25
. ECJ. EECC v UK (Water Supply Regulation, 1993) 46
. ECJ. EECC v UK (Quality of Bathing Water 1992) 47
. ECJ. Advanced Nuclear Fuels GamH v EECC (1992) 60
. ECJ. Vesseso v Zanetti, 22, 23
. Feltham Magistrates Court. Hounslow Trading Standards Authority v Everest (1994) 46
. HC. Anti-Noise Campaign c DoT (29.9.93) 42
. HC. Elizabeth Regina v Ministry of Defence (1993) 34
. HC. Greenpeace v BNFL (1993) 33
. HC. Rudy Molinari v Ministry of Defence (1993) 34
. ICJ. Australia and New Zealand v France (Nuclear Tests 1970) 16, 77
. ICJ. Barcelona Tracton (1970) 16, 77

- 134 -

Index

- ICJ. UK v Albania (Corfu Case 1949) 15, 16, 77
- QBD. Regina v Secretary of State for the Environment Ex Parte Friends of the Earth and Another (29.3.94) 46, 47
- QBD. Regina v Secretary of State for Transport Ex Part Borough of Richmond 42, 43
- Smetler US v Canada (Arbitral Sentence) 15

Charter of Rights and Duties of States 17
Chernobyl 43
Christianity 7
Climate Change 1, 5, 13, 14, 54, 82
Compensation 82, 83, 84
Convention(s), (see also Protocol and Treaties)
- BDC (Biodiversity) 51, 53, 55, 80, 82
- - on Civil Liability for Oil Pollution Damage (Brussels 1969) 61, 78
- - on Civil Liability for Nuclear Damage (Vienna) 71
- - on Civil Liability from Activitites Dangerous to the Environment (CoE) 78
- CCC (Climate Change) 18, 51, 52, 53, 54, 55, 56, 69, 78, 79
- - on Control of Transboundary Movements of Hazardous Wastes and their Disposal, (Basel 22.3.89) 64, 65
- - on Long Range Transboundary Air Pollution
- Pollution of the Ozone Layer (Vienna) 57, 58
- (Hague): - on Peaceful Settlement of International Disputes (1907) 78
- Law of the Sea - 76, 77, 78 79, 80, 81
- - on Prevention of Pollution of Sea by Oil 1954 (London) 61
- - on Prohibition of the Development, Production and Stockpiling of Bacteriological (Biological) and Toxic Weapons and on their Destruction (10.11.72) 65
- - on Protection of the Ozone Layer (Vienna, March 1985) 51, 59
- - on Relating to International Intervention on the High Seas in Cases of Oil Pollution Casualties (Brussels) 61, 78, 82

Conservation of Nature 51, 65
CoE (Council of Europe) 48, 57, 58, 77
Court(s)
- CA (Court of Appeal) 25, 33, 37
- HC (High Court) 33, 34, 42
- ECJ (European Court of Justice) 21, 23, 46, 47, 52, 67, 81

- ICJ (International Court of Justice) 15, 16, 76, 78, 79, 80
- QBD (Queen's Bench Division) 42, 46, 47

Developing Countries 6, 39, 48, 54, 55, 56, 63
DoE 24, 31, 37, 41, 42, 48
Dumping 51, 56, 73, 74
- Control of - 74, 75
- International Conventions on Dumping 75, 76
- Land - 74
- Sea - 74

Earth (Mother) 10, 11, 12, 13, 55, 59, 67, 68
ECA Economic Commission for Africa 51
Ecology 68, 87
Ecologists 10
EEC 17, 21, 31, 42, 44, 51, 52, 53, 60, 63, 64, 76
EECC 41, 46, 47, 63
EEC Directive(s) 35
- - on **Air Protection from Pollution** 52
- - on Dangerous Substances 52
- - on Drinking Water 52
- - on Hazardous Waste 57
- - on Lead in the Air 52
- - on Nitrate 52
- - on Ozone 52, 57
- - on Product Liability 40
- - on Protection of Workers from Noise 41
- - on Protection of Workers from Risks Relating to Exposure to Biological Agents at Work 35
- - on Quality of Bathing Water 52
- - on Reduction of Emmission of Gases 58
- - on Sulphur 52
- - onUrban Waste 52
- - on Waste Movement 52
- - on Work Environment 34
- - on Work Place 35

EEC Law 34, 41, 42
EECT (Rome) 37, 46, 47
Environmental Contamination 23
Environmental Cooperation 13, 14
Environmental Protection 10, 24
Environmental Technologies 52, 55
Erga Omnes Effect 10, 16

FAO 16, 50, 51, 65
Food 10, 20, 32, 37, 38, 39, 44
Food Chains
- Safeway 2
- Sainsbury's 2

Index

- Somerfield (Gateway) 2
- Tesco 2, 32
- Waitrose 2

Food Law 38
Food Security 39, 40,
Food Technology 39
France 32, 41, 43, 44

GATT 16, 51
General Assembly (GA) 50, 68, 69
Germany 32, 59
Ghali (Boutros) UNSG 2
Global Environment Monitoring System 58
God 6, 7, 12
Greek Philosophy 6
Greenhouse Gas(es) 58, 67, 68
Green Movement(s) 1, 18, 19

Habitat 19, 20, 21, 37, 87
Hackney Council 42
Heseltine (Michael) 48
Hounslow Borough Council 44
Hounslow Environmental Charter 43, 44
Howard (Michael) 48

ILO 35
ILO Code of Practice on Safety and Health in Construction Industries 35
IMO 16, 51
Individual(s) 47, 48
International Atomic Energy Agency 68, 71, 72
International Economic Order 54, 55
International Legal Norms 15, 16
Intellectual Property 54, 55
Intellectual Property Rights 54, 55, 66
IPCC 51

Japan 24

Koran (Cow - Al Bakara) Surat 8

Law
- Customary - 16, 27, 76, 78, 81
- Divine - 6
- Environmental - 1, 3, 15, 16, 19, 20, 42, 43, 50, 51, 52
- International - 10, 15, 16, 20, 42, 47, 48, 49, 50, 51, 56, 67, 69, 73, 77, 78
- National - 21, 24, 30, 31, 48, 69, 73,
- Positive - 9, 10, 15

- of the Sea 76, 77, 80

Legal System of Liability 76, 77, 78
Lex Fori 30, 80

Miss London (Magazine) 42
Mediation 78
Moslem Religion 8

National Westminster Bank 32, 48
Negotiation 78
Newspaper(s)
- Independent 32
- Informer 42, 43, 46
- Leader 43
- TLR 25, 41, 46

NGO(s) 14, 52
NNR 21
Noise 19, 41
Nuclear Clouds 67
Nuclear Contamination 10, 23, 56, 66, 67, 70
Nuclear Reactor 66, 70, 71, 72
Nuclear Safety 68, 70, 71
Nuclear Science 67
Nuclear Test(s) 51, 56, 65, 66, 69
Nuclear Waste 23, 67, 68
Nuclear Weapons 51, 66, 67
Nuisance 19, 41

OAU 51, 52, 57
OECD 51, 52
Ozone Layer 51, 57, 58, 59, 66, 69
Ozone Protection 51, 59

Patents 55
Planning 31, 32
Pollution 1, 4, 18, 19, 43, 44, 57
- Air - 18, 43, 50, 57, 58
- Sea - 18, 31, 60, 61, 62, 63
- Land - 18, 63, 64
- International Conventions on Sea - 61
- Preservation of Living Resources 20
- Protection of Consumers 37, 40
- Protection of Wild Birds 20
- Protection of Wildlife 19, 20

Protocol(s) 78
- (Cairo 1964) 78, 79
- Kuwait Protocol Concerning Regional Cooperation Combating Pollution by Oil and Other Harmful Substancs in Cases of Emergency (27.4.1978) - 61
- Radiation 23, 36, 66, 68, 69

Index

- Recycling 31, 32
- Regulation of Disputes 78
- Rig Veda 6
- Rio Declaration 3, 14, 49
- Rio Summit 50, 51, 53
- Rivers 45

SACEP 52
Scandanavia 57
Space Objects 71
State(s) 56, 60, 63, 66, 67, 74
State's Responsibility 81
State's Jurisdiction 18, 72, 75, 76
Stockholm Declaration on Human Environment 2, 13, 14, 16, 33, 50, 51
Strong (Maurice) SG UNCED 49
Surrey County Council 26

Technology 53, 54, 55, 69
- Access to - 54
- Technological Cooperation 53
- Technological Data 54
- Technological Exchange 28, 29, 30, 55
- Transfer of - 39, 54, 58

Third World 39, 48, 62, 63, 64, 65
Third Party Liability 29, 71
Treaty(ies)
- (See Conventions also)
  - on Banning Nuclear Weapon Tests in the Atmosphere, in Outer Space and Under Water (Moscow 5.8.1963) 67
  - Maastricht - 31, 32, 34, 52, 53
    - On Non Proliferation of Nuclear Weapons 68
    - On the Principles Governing the Activities of States in the Exploration and Use of the Outer Space, Including the Moon and Other Celestial Bodies 67
    - On the Prohibition of the Emplacement of Nuclear Weapons and Other Weapons of Mass Destruction on the Sea-Bed and Ocean Floor and the Subsoil Thereof 69

UK 11, 15, 19, 20, 46, 69
UN 2, 3, 14, 15, 24, 39, 41, 43, 49, 50, 51
UN Charter 78, 79
UNCED 3, 11, 12, 16, 49, 50, 51, 52, 53, 54
UNCOD 51
UNEP 16, 17, 50, 51, 65
UNESCO 51

Universal Action 52
US 15, 24, 32, 68
USSR (Russia) 68, 70

Waste 21, 23, 24, 64
- - Authorities 25, 26
- Control of - 24, 25, 26
- - Damage 27, 28, 29
- Disposal of - 21, 22, 24, 25, 26, 27, 28, 31

Water 44, 45, 46, 47
WCIP 16, 51
WHO 65
WMO 16
World Commission on Environment and Development (WCED) 39, 40
World Charter for Nature 17, 50
WTO World Trade Organization 55, 92

Yeltsin (President) 69

International Law Series
Edited and Published by Jalil KASTO

Presents good legal culture and original and up to date studies on the new development of international law and international affairs to the reader. It reflects important and different interests and subjects which are useful to any readers. The first two books are:-

(1)
INTERNATIONAL LAW OF TECHNOLOGY
ISBN 0 9517713 0 2

- It is an original study of technology and its impact on international law and the development of this new law, through UN, international organizations and the practice of the States.
- It deal with transfer of technology, intellectual property rights, patents and computer law and its programmes and other important subjects.
- You find also the **UNCTAD Code of Conduct on the Transfer of Technology** in the book.

(2)
JUS COGENS AND HUMANITARIAN LAW
ISBN 0 9517713 1 0

- It deals with jus cogens (mandatory rules of international law) and humanitarian law and their relation with each other.
- It reflects the new development of humanitarian law and the intervention of the UN for humanitarian aid, e.g. in Iraq, Bosnia and Somalia and the effect and impact of humanitarian aid on international law.
- Also the book deals with the Refugees Problem, and the New UN Conventions on the Ban of Chemical Weapons.

This Series presents to the reader the best quality and interesting books

You can get a copy from the Law Bookshops and international booksellers or contact the publisher:

67 Lyncroft Gardens, Hounslow, Middx TW3 2QU, United Kingdom
Tel. 081-898 2980